AA

Glovebox Guide

INDUSTRIAL HERITAGE OF BRITAIN

Barrie Trinder

Produced by the Publishing Division
of The Automobile Association

4

Editor: *Roger Thomas*
Art Editor: *Harry Williams FCSD*
Illustrations: *John Banbury*
            Delyth Lloyd
Cover picture: *Mary Evans Picture Library*
Typesetting: *Afal, Cardiff*
Printing: *Purnell Book Production Ltd, a member of the*
            BPCC Group

Produced by the Publishing Division of
The Automobile Association

Distributed in the United Kingdom by the
Publishing Division of The Automobile
Association, Fanum House, Basingstoke,
Hampshire RG21 2EA

ISBN 0 86145 684 X

Published by The Automobile Association

INDUSTRIAL HERITAGE OF BRITAIN

Contents

INTRODUCTION

Britain was the world's first industrial nation. Between 1750 and 1850 there were far-reaching changes in the ways in which our ancestors made their livings, and the impact these changes had on everyday life was enormous. The landscape in many parts of Britain was completely transformed. Towns grew rapidly — the population of Birmingham for example grew from 71,000 in 1801 to 233,000 in 1851, while Bradford, a place of little consequence in 1801, with only 13,000 inhabitants, was the metropolis of the woollen industry with a population of 104,000 in 1851. New features appeared in the landscape. Cotton mills, navigable canals, a growing passenger railway network and steam winding engines at coal mines, all commonplace by 1851, would have seemed totally strange to a British person living a century earlier.

CONTINUING REVOLUTION

The process of change did not stop in the mid-19th century. During the first stage of what historians have for many years described as the Industrial

An employee at one of Glasgow's railway works

Revolution, many of the primary stages of manufacture were transformed. It became possible to make iron, cotton or woollen cloth, or glass on a larger scale but most of the goods which people actually used — clothing, tools, furniture or foodstuffs — were still made by individual craftsmen. From the mid-19th century onwards more of the things we use have been made in factories, many of them today coming from factories in distant parts of the world. The Industrial Revolution continues but it has now developed into an international phenomenon.

The remains of the first Industrial Revolution which we can see all over Britain have a very special place in our

Above: *An early pithead and steam winding engine*
Middle: *Traditional weaving skills are kept alive in places like south-west Wales*
Bottom: *A locomotive built at Glasgow*

history, for they are unique to this country. Awe-inspiring cathedrals, elegant country houses and formidable castles are to be found in most European countries. Britain alone is richly blessed in monuments of the first stages of those changes which led to today's industrialised world.

MANUFACTURES AND MINING IN 1700

No one in 1700 would have called Britain an industrial country; indeed the word 'industry' was not then used in its present sense. Nevertheless, both Britons and foreigners recognised that this was a country in which trade and manufactures flourished. Many rivers had been improved so that they could be used by commercial shipping, although there were no artificial canals of the kind which had already been constructed in France. Small seaports all round the coast were busy with commerce and trading.

In many areas fabrics were made which were sold nationally. Exeter was famous for serges, Colchester for baize and Bridport for sailcloth. Around Sheffield, and in the area between Birmingham and Wolverhampton which was to gain the name of the 'Black Country', there were concentrations of craftsmen who produced knives, axes, scythes, locks and nails. The ironworks in the Weald provided cannon for the army and the navy, and at one of them the iron railings were cast for St Paul's Cathedral. Britain had ample supplies of coal, and from its richest coalfield in Northumberland and Durham ships

Yorkshire factory children of the early 19th century

Manufacturing on a grand scale: JJ Colman's great Carrow mustard works complex at Norwich, about 1857

carried the precious source of energy to places all round the eastern and southern coasts.

From the mid-18th century manufacturing in Britain began to expand rapidly. The population began to grow steadily, providing both a labour force and consumers. Entrepreneurs took advantage of improvements in technology, low interest rates and favourable trading opportunities to establish new businesses and expand old ones. Transport facilities were transformed.

Brunel's Moorswater Viaduct near Liskeard, Cornwall, replaced in 1881

Britain, in the space of little more than half a century, became the 'workshop of the world'.

COAL

Coal was the essential source of energy in the first stages of the Industrial Revolution. In many parts of the country transport costs made it too expensive to be used in people's homes in 1700, wood and furze being burned instead. One of the greatest changes which came about in the next 150 years was the growth of canals and railways

Cornish coopers making barrels for china clay

Extensive pithead installations at one of the collieries at Ashington, Northumberland, circa 1900

which made coal available to almost every household.

Coal was being mined in most of the best-known coalfield areas by 1700 — in south Wales, the West Riding, Nottinghamshire, north and south Staffordshire, Lancashire, Shropshire and the Forest of Dean. The coalfield of Northumberland and Durham was the most productive, with the deepest mines and spectacular staithes along the rivers Tyne and Wear where coal was transferred from wooden railways to ships which carried it to London and other ports.

Many coal mines in 1700 were adits, ie passages driven into the sides of hills to reach the coal seams. A real adit is preserved at Beamish (page 83) and there is a reconstructed example at Ironbridge (page 75). Many miners worked 'bell pits', shallow shafts from the bases of which coal was extracted on all sides. When the pit began to collapse the miners would sink another

Beamish's North of England Open-Air Museum is an extensive site which covers many aspects of industrial and social history. This colliery engine house contains a steam winding engine of 1855

nearby, and the bell pit became a damp, saucer-shaped depression. The remains of bell pits can still be seen. The most accessible are those on Catherton Common in the Clee Hills coalfield, just off the A4117 Ludlow—Kidderminster road.

Deeper mines were always in danger from flooding, and in 1712 Thomas Newcomen built the first working steam engine to pump out mines near Dudley. Within little more than two decades there were a hundred such engines in Britain. The early steam engines could produce only an up and down pumping motion, but by the 1780s they were being adapted to turn machines, and many were installed to wind coal from pits. It was not until well into the 19th century that cages were generally installed, which enabled miners to go to and from their work in relative safety. Other new

safety features included steam-driven fans used to circulate fresh air. Most of the preserved collieries in Britain reflect the practice of the 19th or early 20th centuries, but they nevertheless convey much of the atmosphere of earlier periods of mining (see Heads of the Valleys Road page 57 and Caphouse page 89).

USERS OF COAL

Wherever coal was mined industries which used it tended to develop. Many of them made use of the clays found in association with coal. Bricks were made in many parts of Britain. By the 19th century the demands of London builders were such that large numbers of bricks were being made for them in the Medway Valley in Kent and in Bedfordshire.

The north Staffordshire coalfield was already an important pottery-making area in 1700, but from the mid-18th century the industry was

A 19th-century view of an ironworks near Shifnal, Shropshire (probably the furnaces at Stirchley, now in Telford Town Park)

organised on a factory basis, the most celebrated of the new concerns being Josiah Wedgwood's Etruria, built on the banks of the Trent and Mersey Canal in 1769 (see Stoke-on-Trent page 80). In the 19th century the 'five towns' of the Potteries (actually six) were notorious as one of the most polluted districts in Britain, due to the thick smoke produced by hundreds of the 'bottle ovens' in which pottery was fired.

The making of glass also involved the use of large amounts of coal. The most characteristic structures of the industry were the 'English' glass cones, conical buildings up to 16m in diameter and up to 25m high, but many processes were carried out in buildings of more conventional appearance. Bristol and Tyneside were both important glass-producing areas in 1700, but by the mid-19th century the St Helens region of Lancashire was the leading producer of flat glass, and Stourbridge in the West Midlands (page 81) was the main centre for decorative wares.

SIMPLIFIED CROSS-SECTION OF AN ENGLISH GLASS CONE

Glass is made by fusing silica (sand) with soda and other ingredients at high temperature

A *The cone*
B *The chimney at the apex*
C *Entrances through arches in the side*
D *The furnace*
E *Flues to the furnace*
F *The pots holding molten glass*
G *Annealing hearths set in the sides of the cone*

Making salt from brine was a trade which was similarly concentrated on the coalfields. It was an important industry on the Tyne in the early 18th century, but the 'wich' towns of Cheshire (see Northwich page 98) have been the principal centres in more recent times, and salt production has become the basis of a number of major chemical enterprises.

Eighteenth- and 20th-century industrial monuments at Lemington, Newcastle upon Tyne: an English glass cone, in front of the cooling towers of a power station

IRON

The increase in the production of iron in the 18th and 19th centuries was one of the most far-reaching of the changes brought by the Industrial Revolution. In the early 18th century British furnaces were producing in the region of 25,000 tons of iron a year. By the end of the century annual output had risen about ten times, and it again increased tenfold in the next 50 years.

Iron was smelted from iron ore in blast furnaces. In 1700 all British furnaces used charcoal as their fuel, but supplies were limited, and a dramatic increase in production could not be envisaged. In 1709 at Coalbrookdale Abraham Darby first smelted iron with coke. From the 1750s the process was widely adopted and for a time the area around Coalbrookdale and the Ironbridge Gorge was the most important iron-producing region in Britain (see Ironbridge page 75), but by the end of the 18th century it was being displaced by the Black Country and south Wales where the mineral resources were much greater.

An early iron forge at Tintern, south-east Wales

BLAST FURNACE

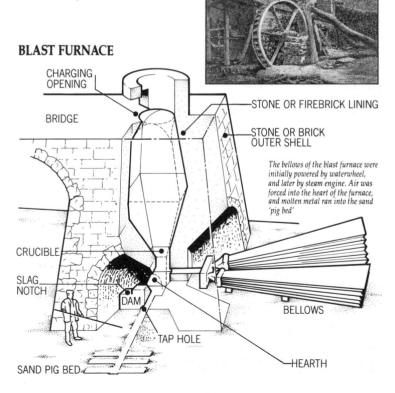

CHARGING OPENING

BRIDGE

STONE OR FIREBRICK LINING

STONE OR BRICK OUTER SHELL

The bellows of the blast furnace were initially powered by waterwheel, and later by steam engine. Air was forced into the heart of the furnace, and molten metal ran into the sand 'pig bed'

CRUCIBLE

SLAG NOTCH

DAM

BELLOWS

TAP HOLE

SAND PIG BED

HEARTH

A blast furnace was a substantial brick or stone structure whose interior resembled two cones or pyramids placed base to base. Raw materials were fed in at the top, and molten iron let out into the open moulds of a 'pig bed' (so called because it was said to resemble pigs feeding from a sow) twice a day. Air was supplied from bellows worked first by waterwheels, then from the 1770s by steam engines.

A blast furnace produced cast iron which could be remelted to make castings. Cast iron has a carbon content of about 4 per cent. The greatest demand was for wrought iron, ie iron free of carbon, which could be used for tools and nails. The most commonly used method of making wrought iron from pig iron was puddling, invented by Henry Cort in 1784.

Steel is the name applied to forms of iron with a carbon content between that of wrought and cast iron, often with traces of other elements. In the 18th century steel was used for swords, the edges of scythes and similar purposes. It was made in cementation furnaces, or from 1740 by the crucible process invented by Benjamin Huntsman. In the 1850s Sir Henry Bessemer developed mild steel, which had some of the properties of both cast and wrought iron, and is the material from which motor cars and countless other items in daily use are still made. In addition to the Ironbridge entry, iron and steel production is described at other sites in this book, notably the Heads of the Valleys Road (page 57), Duddon (page 90) and Bonawe (page 105).

IRON PUDDLING FURNACE
(CUT OPEN TO SHOW INTERIOR)

This puddling furnace converted the iron produced by the blast furnace (see previous page) into better-quality wrought iron

LIFTING LEVER

CHIMNEY

FIREBRIDGE

FIREBRICK WALLS AND ARCHED ROOF

OUTER CASING

STOKE-HOLE

FIREPLACE

RABBLE

ASH PIT

BALL BOGIE

FLUE

BOWL

TAP HOLE

TONGS

Ruins of 18th-century blast furnaces at Hirwaun, south Wales, one of the first coke-using ironworks in Wales

OTHER METALS

The production of other metals was also of great importance during the Industrial Revolution. Tin had been mined in Cornwall since prehistoric times, and lead working was an old-established occupation in the Pennines.

During the 18th century Britain became one of the world's leading producers of copper. Most metallic ores were found in fissures in older rocks, and not in seams like coal and most forms of iron ore. Mining was therefore less certain. Most mines were at a distance from sources of coal so that the operation of steam engines for pumping and winding was expensive. At old lead or copper mines you can expect to see evidence of steam engine houses, compressor plants which provided air to work drills, machines for crushing ore, and extensive dressing floors where the ore was separated from the lighter elements with which it was mixed (see Magpie Mine page 77).

A works (1792) in the Greenfield Valley, Holywell, north Wales, in which copper sheets were rolled and copper bolts for ships were formed

TEXTILES

The manufacture of textiles was one of the fastest-growing industries in 18th-century Britain, and in most countries which have subsequently undergone industrialisation the making of fabrics has been one of the first activities to be organised on a factory basis. Textile manufacture was important in most parts of Britain at the beginning of the 18th century, but it was universally undertaken on a domestic basis, with clothiers co-ordinating the production of many homes. The first textile 'factory' was a water-powered mill for throwing silk, built, following Italian precedents, by John Lombe, in Derby in about 1717. It became a celebrated building, visited by many tourists.

The first water-powered cotton-spinning factory was constructed by Richard Arkwright, a wig-maker, born in Preston, who was responsible for setting to work the 'water-frame', a machine for spinning cotton yarn. He operated a factory using horse-power in Nottingham from 1769 but two years later moved to the isolated village of Cromford (page 72) in Derbyshire, where there was ample water power. It was completed in 1771, and within 20 years it had become just one of a group of buildings devoted to the production and storage of cotton yarn. In 1784—5 Arkwright constructed another complex in Cromford around Masson Mill, a building of great elegance, rather like a flagship announcing his success as a manufacturer. Arkwright

Men, women and children operating spinning mules in the 1840s

was a partner in many other cotton-spinning enterprises in Derbyshire and elsewhere.

It was more difficult to work looms mechanically, and many weavers continued to use hand looms in their own homes well into the 19th century. Large numbers of weavers' cottages with traditional long-light windows can still be seen on either side of the Pennines. By the 1840s most cotton was made in mill complexes. Most processes were concentrated in 5- or 6-storey buildings, but others, like fulling or dyeing, were often carried out in

Late 19th-century weaving sheds with their unusual roof line and small, north-facing windows

Multi-storeyed cotton works sprung up in the late 18th and early 19th centuries

single-storey accommodation, or in specialist structures like the round drying stoves characteristic of the West of England woollen region. As larger machines were developed in the mid-19th century some branches of the trade, like jute manufacture in Dundee, utilised many single-storey buildings, while from the 1860s weaving sheds, with dog-tooth roofs and windows on the northern sides designed to keep out the dazzle of direct sunlight, became common features of most textile regions.

The industrial revolution in cotton manufacture began in the East Midlands, but by the early 19th century the greatest concentration of mills was in Lancashire, where the industry continued to grow until World War I. The West Riding of Yorkshire was already a well-established wool-manufacturing area in 1700, and became by far the most important centre of the industry by the mid-19th century (see Bradford page 84, and Leeds page 93).

The fortunes of other woollen areas varied. The industry ceased to be of any significance around Colchester, Exeter and Norwich, but in Gloucestershire and Wiltshire factories were built and the trade remained relatively prosperous. Linen manufacture also underwent an industrial revolution, the entrepreneur most largely responsible being John Marshall of Leeds, the city which became the principal centre for the trade. Silk manufacture moved from London in the course of the 18th century, and was established at Macclesfield and Congleton in Cheshire together with Middleton in Lancashire.

TRANSPORT

Transport was revolutionised between 1750 and 1850. Places like Shrewsbury or York, from which in 1750 it took two or three days to reach London along roads which were scarcely made up, were within five or six hours of the capital by train in 1850. The system of navigable rivers, which already extended to many English towns in the early 18th century, was developed from the early 1760s by the construction of canals. By 1820 there

Canal folk decorated not only their barges, but also their pots and pans

The narrow canal of the English Midlands, with its gaily painted boats, its bridges and its wharves became one of the most characteristic features of the landscape of the Industrial Revolution. The seaports were transformed, as wet docks were constructed in which ships could safely float at any state of the tide, often fringed with warehouses, and surrounded by high walls to give a measure of security against theft.

The Rochdale Canal near Littleborough. Such waterways were carried through the hills to create a network which linked together much of industrial Britain

were few towns of consequence in the southern half of Britain which were more than a few miles from navigable water of some kind. Many canals were built to serve purely local needs, but the waterways system as a whole contributed to reducing costs by making coal more generally available throughout Britain, so encouraging manufactures of many kinds.

This system also provided a means of distribution for small consignments from any part of the country to any other within a few days.

Cardiff's Bute West Dock, crowded with tall-masted vessels in the 1870s

Roads were also transformed. In the 1660s there began the development of a system which transferred the costs of main roads from those who happened to live in the parishes through which they ran to those who used them. Parliament authorised the establishment of bodies of trustees who were empowered to collect tolls from road users at gates (or turnpikes).

Such roads became known as turnpike roads, and to bring a road under this type of legislation came to be described as 'turnpiking'. Only a few roads had been turnpiked by 1700, but within the next 50 years most of the principal radial routes from London to the chief provincial cities were turnpikes, and by the end of the century there were tollhouses on almost every road of consequence. In the early 19th century turnpike trusts were responsible for constructing many entirely new stretches of road. Many tollhouses built by such trusts remain, together with the mileposts which the trusts were obliged to erect alongside their roads.

Right and below right, plans for tollhouses to be placed along Thomas Telford's Holyhead Road. Below, at Llanfair PG on the Isle of Anglesey, the architect's intentions were quite faithfully expressed by the builders

Railways in England originated around 1600. They were used in coalfields, to transport coal from pits to navigable water, and two distinct systems grew up — in Shropshire, and in Northumberland and County Durham. In Shropshire during the 18th century iron wheels were used on waggons, and from 1767 iron rails were employed. In 1802 the first steam railway locomotive was built at Coalbrookdale although it was not successfully put to use. After that date the principal developments were in the north-east. The T-section wrought-iron rail was perfected by James Birkinshaw at Bedlington ironworks in 1820, and the steam locomotive was gradually

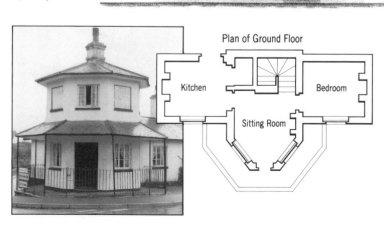

Plan of Ground Floor

Kitchen

Bedroom

Sitting Room

developed by George Stephenson and others. In many parts of the country in the first three decades of the 19th century so-called 'hybrid' railways were built, with some sections worked by horses, some by steam locomotives and some by inclined planes.

The Liverpool and Manchester Railway, opened in 1830 and engineered by George Stephenson, was the first main-line railway in the modern sense. Its tracks were entirely separated from public roads, and its trains were hauled by steam locomotive. It was subject to parliamentary control, and open to all forms of traffic, both passengers and goods. By 1851 over 6,000 miles of railway had been built on the same principles, and passenger stations, goods depots, viaducts, cuttings and embankments had become familiar parts of the British landscape.

Top: *The South-Eastern Railway's Cannon Street terminus, London, opened in 1866*
Above: *The transport revolution continued with the introduction of London's 'tube' trains*

The magnificent viaduct, built for the Great Northern Railway's main line, spanning the valley of the River Mimram near Welwyn

INDUSTRIAL COMMUNITIES

The concentration of manufactures into larger units during the Industrial Revolution led to the growth of new kinds of communities. Some were scattered and untidy settlements which were often created by squatters who built their own houses on common land near to sources of employment. It is possible to see this kind of informal settlement in parts of the Black Country (see Dudley page 74), in the Forest of Dean (page 31) or in the Clee Hills in Shropshire, and many of the textile communities on either side of the Pennines share these characteristics. Other settlements were built by the great entrepreneurs of the Industrial Revolution for their workers.

Silk weavers' attics extend above the general roof line of Macclesfield's Pitt Street, which retains its cobbles and 19th-century frontage

Three-storey cottages, part of Richard Arkwright's factory village at Cromford

At the best preserved of them, Cromford, Coalbrookdale, Saltaire and New Lanark, it is possible to see not just the houses erected for workers and their families, but schools, institutes, places of worship, and in some cases pubs, parks and hospitals. The Industrial Revolution also brought about the concentration of much of the population in towns and cities. Much of the housing built before the late 19th century has now been demolished, but in recent years historians have come to appreciate that every major city and region had its own style of house. In Newcastle this was the two-storey flat, in Leeds the brick-built back-to-back, in Liverpool the enclosed back-to-back court, in Sunderland the single-storey terrace. In London high land values led charitable bodies to build blocks of apartments, of four, five or six storeys, to accommodate working people whose jobs tied them to the city centre.

HEALTHIER LIVING

During the 1830s and 40s people in public life came to realise that living conditions in many parts of Britain were far from healthy, that many people were permanently ill, and many died from the lack of drainage, from polluted water supplies and generally inadequate housing. The squalor of some parts of rapidly growing industrial cities like Manchester was spectacular, and served to draw attention to the problems, but sober enquiries showed that conditions in smaller towns and in many rural areas were almost as bad.

One of the Victorians' great achievements was to make Britain a healthier place in which to live. From the passing of the Public Health Act in 1848, many towns were drained through networks of sewers, and new supplies of clean water were provided.

Drainage as an art form at London's highly decorative Abbey Mills Pumping Station

New houses could only be built if they conformed to standards imposed by Boards of Health. While much squalor remained by 1900, the basis of healthier living conditions had been created. The most spectacular memorials to this process are the steam engines built for pumping sewage or drinking water, many of which have been preserved. The spectacular architecture and ornate settings of such engines as those at Papplewick (see Nottingham page 78), Ryhope (page 99) and Abbey Mills (see London page 41) show how the Victorians appreciated the extent of the far-reaching changes which they were bringing about.

ABOUT THIS BOOK

This book is an introduction to the monuments of the Industrial Revolution, that great change in British society which occurred between 1700 and 1900. There are many important industrial archaeological sites which date from before 1700, and even more 20th-century industrial buildings which are of interest, but we shall confine our attention here to a selection of the outstanding monuments which remain from the time when Britain became the first industrial nation. All the places described here can be visited. Some are museums or places which are formally conserved, and may therefore be accessible only during limited opening hours. Some are still working industrial premises, to which the public are not admitted, although they are only mentioned if they are worth seeing without any need to trespass. There are several recommended 'rides' through areas where a drive (or walk) is the best way to appreciate the industrial landscape and its various sites.

THE WEST COUNTRY

The scarring effects of Cornwall's china clay industry

*T*he west of England has a long and proud industrial past. The tin mines of Cornwall have been worked since prehistoric times, but the Royal Duchy was rather more important during the Industrial Revolution as a source of copper. The industrial landscapes created by the mining of metals around Redruth and Camborne and by china clay workings near St Austell are some of the most dramatic in Britain.

Events in Cornwall influenced the growth of industry elsewhere. The 'five towns' of the north Staffordshire Potteries would never have grown so quickly without china clay from Cornwall, nor would copper smelting have become established in Swansea. Without the demand for efficient steam power from the mines of Cornwall, James Watt's development of the steam engine in Birmingham would have followed a different course. Woollen cloth was manufactured in many parts of the west of England before the late 18th century. In Devon the industry rapidly declined, but in Wiltshire and Gloucestershire clothiers went over to the factory system and built the elegant mills which still remain. The west of England is also celebrated for its overseas trade and the ports of Bristol and Gloucester are as rich in historical monuments as any in Britain.

BATH, *Avon*

Bath is one of the most elegant of European cities, a spa and resort with remarkable Roman antiquities, where well-proportioned houses in the superb local stone were erected in the 18th and early 19th centuries to accommodate those who had made or inherited moderate fortunes.

The Kennet and Avon Canal which passes along the southern side of the city from its junction with the River Avon was opened in 1810. The canal climbs out of the Avon Valley by means of the flight of six (formerly seven) locks at Widcombe. At the top of the lock flight is Baird's Maltings, dating from the 1850s, where malt was made by traditional methods until 1972. Most of the building is now converted into offices, with a house incorporated into the one-time malt kiln. In Sydney Gardens the canal is crossed by two small iron bridges provided by the Coalbrookdale Company in 1800. Brunel's Great Western Railway runs parallel to the canal. The most magnificent feature of

the Kennet and Avon Canal is John Rennie's Dundas Aqueduct 3 miles south of Bath, which walkers can reach by following the towpath. It can be approached by car east of the A36 a mile south of Claverton.

Bath has several interesting bridges, the most important of them being the Pulteney Bridge over the Avon, which is lined with shops and was built by Robert Adam in 1769. The Victoria Bridge is a suspension bridge of 37m span built in 1836 to an unusual design patented by James Dredge, a local engineer. The Cleveland Bridge of 1827 is an iron arch cast by William Hazledine of Shrewsbury.

Bath is rich in museums. The one most closely linked with industrial history is the Bath Industrial Heritage Centre which houses the tools, equipment and stock-in-trade of J B Bowler who established an engineering business in Corn Street in 1872. When the firm ceased operation in 1969 the lathes, patterns and hand tools were transferred to the museum.

The Kennet and Avon Canal crosses the River Avon by the Dundas Aqueduct

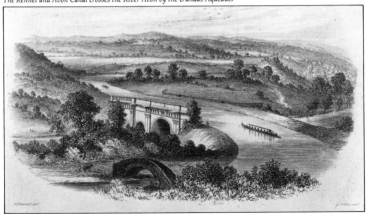

Wheal Coates, an old Cornish tin mine in spectacular coastal setting near St Agnes Head north-east of Redruth

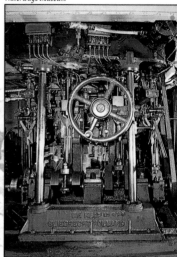

A steam dredger on display at Gloucester's National Waterways Museum

The 'moonscapes' that have been created by St Austell's china clay industry

Embellishment on the SS Great Britain, *the historic iron-hulled ship moored at Bristol*

Exeter Maritime Museum's attractive location

A cooper at work at Morwellham Quay, where the past is relived

Chatham's dockyards played an important role in the history of naval shipping

There is much to delight steam enthusiasts at the Great Western Railway Museum, Swindon

A blacksmith making the sparks fly at the Amberley Chalk Pits Museum

Top: *Re-created cottage scene in the Forest of Dean's Heritage Centre*
Middle: *The waterwheels at Gloucestershire's Stanley Mill were once powered by this rushing water course*
Bottom: *This portrait of the locomotive* City of Truro *is occasionally displayed in the GWR Museum, Swindon*

BRADFORD-ON-AVON, *Wiltshire*

Bradford is a town of spectacular beauty, rising on the slopes of a gorge above the River Avon. The town's ancient prosperity was based on the manufacture of the celebrated Wiltshire broadcloth. From the late 18th century

The handsome Abbey Mill beside the River Avon

factories were constructed in the county, and by 1850 they accommodated most stages of production. The industry declined by the end of the 19th century, but the mills can still be seen, as they found new life from a 20th-century industry, the making of rubber tyres and hoses. Abbey Mill, completed in 1874, is a magnificent building in the Venetian Gothic style, the centrepiece of Bradford's spectacular river frontage.

Old woollen mills at nearby Melksham are also used by rubber manufacturers, but the most important industrial monuments in the town are two stoves for drying cloth. One, in Lowborne, is octagonal and is now a private house. The other, in Church Street, is circular and serves as the tourist office.

BRISTOL, *Avon*

Bristol's prosperity over many centuries arose from its overseas trade. Although most commercial shipping activity now takes place at Avonmouth and Portishead, the City Docks, created by manipulating the channels of the tidal River Avon, remain some of the most interesting in Britain. The 'floating harbour' was the work of William Jessop in the first decade of the 19th century, and substantial improvements were made to the docks by I K Brunel in the 1840s and Thomas Howard in the 1870s.

It is possible to walk through the dock area from Cumberland Basin, where Jessop's 10m-wide southern lock was enlarged to 17m by Brunel in 1848, past Underfall Yard, where the workshops and hydraulic pumps of the dock system are situated, Wapping Wharf and the Bathurst Basin to Bristol Bridge. A steam crane designed by William Fairbairn and built by Stothert and Pitt of Bath in 1875 is preserved on Wapping Wharf by the Bristol Industrial Museum. The museum itself is in nearby dock buildings, and

The Fairbairn steam crane

provides an introduction to the city's varied industrial history. Many of the warehouse buildings are being adapted to new uses, notably the Arnolfini Gallery in Bush's tea warehouse which dates from around 1830, and the Watershed centre.

Bristol is notable for its links with one of the most idiosyncratic of British engineers, Isambard Kingdom Brunel. The SS *Great Britain*, the world's first screw-driven, iron-hulled ship, was designed by Brunel and launched in 1843 from Wapping Dock where she now reposes, after being brought back from the Falkland Islands in 1970.

Spanning the Avon Gorge, Brunel's magnificent Clifton Suspension Bridge

Brunel also designed the Clifton Suspension Bridge, on which work began in 1836, but the project ran out of money four years later. It was completed between 1861 and 1864 as a memorial to the engineer. Brunel's greatest achievement was the building of the Great Western Railway from Bristol to London, which opened in 1841. Temple Meads Station, the western terminus of the line with its 22m-span hammerbeam roof, is being restored by a charitable trust.

EXETER, *Devon*

Exeter, the county town of Devon was, until the early 19th century, one of the principal centres of the woollen cloth trade. It supplied materials to spinners and weavers over a wide area, and was a centre to which woollen cloth was brought for fulling and dyeing prior to transportation by sea.

From the industrial point of view the most interesting part of the city is the Riverside, near the terminus of the Exeter Canal, constructed in the 16th century to provide a reliable route to the sea. It was in this area just outside the city walls that cloth was hung on tenters to be stretched and dried. The 'leats' (watercourses) which provided water for the waterwheels of the fulling mills can still be seen. The area is dominated by the impressive warehouses built on the quay in the 1830s. The Exeter Maritime Museum, with a collection of sailing craft from all over the world, occupies part of the canal basin. Near to the city centre a delicate iron bridge of 1814 carries a footpath over The Close.

The pretty little iron bridge over The Close, Exeter

FOREST OF DEAN, *Gloucestershire*
The Forest of Dean is the area between the River Wye and the lower Severn, bordered roughly by Monmouth, Cinderford and Chepstow. It is still heavily wooded, and driving through the Forest reveals magnificent woodland scenery. Dean was for many centuries an industrial area, and there are many traces of its coal mines and ironworks and of the tramways and railways which carried their products to the Severn and the Wye. Small, privately operated coal mines remain in use, and in many places it is possible to see how miners built their own cottages in clearings and around the edges of commons.

The best introduction to a tour of the Forest is the Dean Heritage Centre at Soudley. The outstanding

Whitecliff Blast Furnace, built to smelt iron ore

The attractive Dean Heritage Centre

monument of the iron industry in the Forest is Whitecliff Furnace on the lane which runs in a south-westerly direction from Coleford towards the B4231. The furnace was built in 1806, and worked only for a few years. Its stone stack is well preserved and can

easily be seen from the road. At Clearwell Caves, once known as the Old Ham Mine, on the B4228 about 2 miles south of Coleford, it is possible to go underground and see where the iron ore used in furnaces like Whitecliff was mined. At Parkend on the B4431 a blowing engine house built in the early 19th century to provide blast for an iron furnace is now used as a field studies centre.

Lydney Harbour, opened in 1813, was the terminus of the Severn and Wye Railway, a remarkable industrial tramroad which ran across the forest to Lydbrook on the Wye, with many branches serving mines and ironworks. Some stone blocks used as sleepers on the line, and L-shaped plate rails on which the waggons ran have been incorporated into the harbour walls and wharves. At Redbrook there is a steeply inclined bridge built to carry a tramroad across the B4231. A steam centre at Norchard, north of Lydney on the B4234, has a collection of ex-GWR locomotives, and the former Great Western signal box at Tintern on the A466 is preserved as a visitor centre.

GLOUCESTER, *Gloucestershire*

The county town of Gloucestershire was important for many centuries as a transhipment port on the River Severn where goods were transferred from barges which could navigate upstream to Shropshire or mid Wales into larger vessels more suited to the treacherous waters of the estuary. Some boats nevertheless always sailed right through to Bristol without unloading their cargoes. In 1827 the Gloucester and Berkeley Canal was opened linking the city with Sharpness, and by-passing a dangerous section of the lower Severn.

From that time began the growth of Gloucester Docks where many warehouses of the early and mid-19th century still stand, although commercial traffic has now ceased. The North Warehouse bears the inscription 'The Gloucester and Berkeley Canal Company's Warehouse erected by W Rees and Son Ano. Dom. 1826'. The Albert Warehouse contains the fascinating Robert Opie Museum of Packaging and Advertising, and the

One of Robert Opie's cornucopia of icons produced by the consumer age

National Waterways Museum is housed in the Llanthony Warehouse. The Over Bridge of 1831 is one of the most elegant stone bridges built by Thomas Telford.

MORWELLHAM, *Devon*

Morwellham is a river port on the Tamar which flourished in the mid-19th century as an outlet for copper, arsenic, manganese and slate, products which were brought to the riverside and despatched to the sea at Plymouth, 23 miles downstream. The Tamar is for much of its length the boundary between Devon and Cornwall, and Morwellham is the highest point which could be reached by vessels of 3.3m draught. Morwellham's period of prosperity began with the completion of the $4\frac{1}{2}$-mile-long Tavistock Canal in 1817. The end of the canal was 72m above the river, and a 229m-long inclined plane carried goods down to the wharves. For a short time around 1850 the Tamar Valley was the most important source of copper in Europe and Morwellham was very busy. From about 1870 it declined, but a century later restoration began, and visitors can now see the raised railway system around the docks, the inclined plane and the canal tunnel at the top, as well as limekilns and workers' housing. It is even possible to ride a train into one of the copper mines.

Llanthony Warehouse in Gloucester Docks, home of the National Waterways Museum

REDRUTH, *Cornwall*

Redruth is the centre of the copper-
and tin-mining industries which in the
18th and 19th centuries created
dramatic landscapes across much of
west Cornwall. The best viewpoint
from which to appreciate the region is
the de Dunstanville monument on
Carn Brea, a granite tower erected in
1836 in memory of a prominent local
landowner. One of the most distinctive
features of the Cornish industrial
landscape is the Cornish engine house,
built to contain steam engines for
draining mines. More than 300 survive
in the west of England. Several can be
seen from the A30 near Redruth, and
the National Trust cares for houses
which still contain their engines at East
Pool near Redruth. There are
spectacularly placed engine houses on
the coast of St Agnes and Botallack
near St Just. The first Cornish engine
was built by Richard Trevithick at

Miners at work at East Pool, 1893

Wheal Prosper in 1811. Many Cornish
harbours were connected with the
mining industry. That at Portreath is
particularly dramatic, while the
harbour walls at Hayle are made of
slag, the waste product of the local
copper smelters.

On the surface at East Pool at the turn of the century

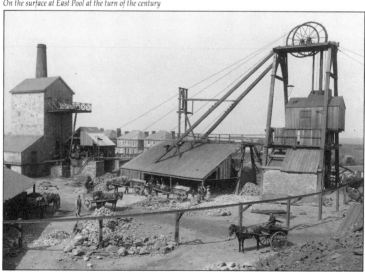

ST AUSTELL, *Cornwall*

Until the early 18th century Europeans could only admire porcelain as something of great beauty which was made exclusively by the Chinese. Eventually it was discovered that the essential ingredient which distinguished it from common earthenware was kaolin, or china clay. Small workshops making porcelain were established in Bow in 1743 and Chelsea in 1744, and the following year William Cookworthy of Plymouth discovered that china clay was to be found in large quantities in Devon and Cornwall. By the 1770s Cornish china clay was being shipped to the north Staffordshire Potteries.

As demand increased during the Industrial Revolution more pits were opened, and in the course of time new uses were found for china clay in papermaking, plastics and pharmaceuticals. St Austell is the centre of the Cornish china clay industry, and the huge tips of waste which dominate the area form one of the most dramatic industrial

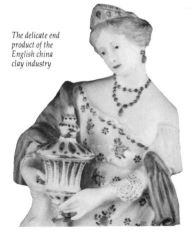

The delicate end product of the English china clay industry

landscapes in Britain, best appreciated from the B3374 south of Bugle or the B3279 south from St Dennis. Ports like Charlestown, built in the early 1790s by John Smeaton for Charles Rashleigh, a local landowner, were developed to handle exports.

Charlestown Harbour, busy with boats

Pentewan, terminus of a 0.75m/2ft 6in-gauge railway, opened in 1826 but long ago lost all its traffic. China clay is now taken by rail to Fowey for export, much of it passing under the spectacular Treffry Viaduct at Luxulyan, built as part of another china clay railway in 1843.

The Wheal Martyn Museum at Carthew on the A391 is located in two old clay works, the earliest of which dates from the 1820s. The whole process of clay extraction and treatment can be followed through the displays and the surviving remains of the works. Exhibits include a 10.5m-diameter working waterwheel used to pump clay slurry from the pit, ranges of settling pits and settling tanks, a pan-kiln for drying clay, the linhay, where dry clay was stored before being taken away to customers, and two locomotives formerly used for china clay traffic. An audio-visual production provides an introduction to the museum, and there is a waymarked walk which includes a visit to a working clay pit.

STROUD VALLEY, *Gloucestershire*

The Stroud Valley was for many centuries important for the manufacture of woollen cloth. From the closing years of the 18th century the manufacture was gradually concentrated in factories. Many remained in production until well into the 20th century and several still make cloth. Most of the mills are of stone construction and they form a dominant feature of the landscape. The majority were originally powered by water, even

The Thames and Severn Canal passed from the Stroud Valley under the Cotswolds by means of the Sapperton Tunnel, opened in 1789

if steam engines were added later, so that they are concentrated along the valley bottoms. The A46 from Nailsworth to Stroud provides a panorama of mills, including the impressive five-storey Dunkirk Mill with its huge millpond. Ebley Mill, which is being converted to offices, was rebuilt by the celebrated Victorian architect G F Bodley. The most splendid of all the Stroudwater mills is that at King's Stanley, built in 1813, with an iron frame and in the most tasteful of classical styles. Woollen cloth is still made at King's Stanley, and there is a factory shop located on the premises.

SWINDON, *Wiltshire*

For 150 years Swindon was a railway town, where the Great Western Railway built and repaired its locomotives and carriages. The town of Swindon was situated a little distance from the station and works, so the railway company built their own village to the design of Matthew Digby

The former Great Western Hospital (centre of photograph) stands close to the turreted Great Western Railway Museum building

Wyatt, architect of Paddington Station, from 1845 onwards. Subsequent commercial development took place around the old town, leaving the company village essentially intact. It was well restored in the 1970s by the local district council.

At the centre is the former Mechanics' Institute, while on the edge is the Church of St Mark, designed by George Gilbert Scott, and one of the favourite churches of the late Sir John Betjeman. A Great Western Museum (with a replica of the locomotive *North Star*, one of the first to run on the Great Western), is situated in a large building which has served as a lodging house for enginemen and also as a chapel. One of the adjacent houses has been restored to its condition at about the turn of the century.

TROWBRIDGE, *Wiltshire*

Until about 1900 Trowbridge was an important centre for woollen cloth manufacture. Many mills have been demolished but enough survive to give an impression of the town's industrial past. Most can be seen during a walk along the banks of the River Biss from the car park near the county hall. Upper Mill is a four-storey, brick-built block of 12 bays fronting the riverside. At Stone Mill, which stands at right angles to the Biss, there are traces of the water-power system, as well as a chimney built when a steam engine was installed in 1814. Studley Mill is notable for its three-storeyed brick building with perforated walls spanning the river, which was used for drying handles, the frames in which teasel heads were mounted (teasel heads are the spiky heads of teasel plants, used to lift up the ends of fibres in cloth so that the fabric could be

A wool store at Melksham, near Trowbridge

sheared). Also within the complex are a late-19th-century building with sheep portrayed in relief panels, and an 18th-century clothier's house. Most west of England woollen mills grew up around the houses of clothiers.

Studley Mill's handle house

SOUTH AND SOUTH-EAST ENGLAND

Water power in action at the Weald and Downland Museum, Singleton

*T*he industrial history of the south-east of England is dominated by London, the country's greatest centre of manufacturing, as well as its seat of government. The trading importance of London gave rise to the growth of the vast system of docks which stretched down the Thames from the Tower to Tilbury by the end of the 19th century, and also brought prosperity to other ports in the south-east which benefited from the easy access which railways afforded to the capital.

Many of the outstanding industrial monuments of the region are connected with the supplying of London. The Kentish brickfields and the limekilns of the Downlands provided building materials for London. The New River was a remarkable enterprise which supplied London with drinking water. The Great Western

Railway was conceived in part as a means of linking London with America, by taking passengers by train to Bristol and thence by steamer across the Atlantic. Naval installations like the dockyards at Sheerness and Chatham were related to the need to defend London from seaborne enemies. The ironworks of the Weald prospered because they had access to customers in London. Nevertheless there were many craftsmen who supplied local needs in the south-east and their skills are splendidly reflected in the Weald and Downland Museum (see page 51).

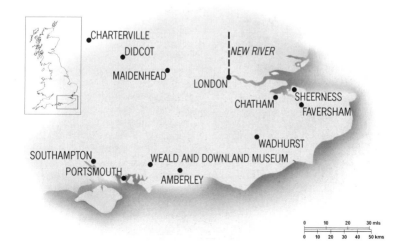

CHARTERVILLE
DIDCOT
MAIDENHEAD
NEW RIVER
LONDON
CHATHAM
SHEERNESS
FAVERSHAM
WADHURST
SOUTHAMPTON
WEALD AND DOWNLAND MUSEUM
PORTSMOUTH
AMBERLEY

| 0 | 10 | 20 | 30 mls |
| 0 | 10 | 20 | 30 | 40 | 50 kms |

AMBERLEY, *West Sussex*

Amberley Chalk Pits Museum is situated on the B2139 near to Amberley Station on the line from Horsham to Littlehampton. It is in part an open-air museum to which various buildings and collections relating to the

Ride into the past at Amberley

industrial history of south-east England have been moved, and in part a site museum, telling the story of the lime-burning enterprises which flourished on the spot for well over a century. The burning of chalk to make lime for building and agricultural purposes had begun at Amberley by 1841, but the earliest kilns were destroyed when the railway was opened in 1863.

Today it is possible to see kilns built not long after this date together with a massive 18-chamber bank of kilns built to a Belgian design in the early years of this century. This is also

Boat-building is one of the old skills which lives on at Amberley

a working museum where craftsmen demonstrate blacksmithing, boat building, wood turning, printing and potting skills. Other sections of the museum deal with narrow-gauge industrial railways, brick-making and road transport. The area just outside the museum, with a turnpike house, the railway and a channel cut off the River Arun for barges collecting lime, is full of interest.

CHARTERVILLE, *Oxfordshire*

Charterville Allotments is the name of a settlement which straggles southwards from Minster Lovell off the A40 between Oxford and Burford. Exploration reveals that many of the cottages are of the same three-bay bungalow design. Charterville was built in 1847 and it takes its name from Chartism which was originally a movement to give more people the vote, through which it was hoped improvements in living conditions would result. Petitions were presented to Parliament in 1839 and 1842, but to no avail, and in 1845 the Chartist Land Company was set up by Feargus O'Connor to enable industrial workers to return to the land. Five estates were purchased with funds raised from subscribers. Cottages of a standardised design were built in four-acre plots and each village was provided with a school. The company collapsed but the school and more than 60 of the original 78 cottages remain at Charterville as evidence of the appeal which the land had for the first generations of industrial workers. The other villages are Heronsgate near Rickmansworth, Snigs End and Lowbands near Tewkesbury, and Dodford just north-west of Bromsgrove.

CHATHAM, *Kent*

The ex-Royal Navy dockyard at Chatham on the River Medway is one of the most important historic industrial sites in Britain. As the yard expanded in the 19th century the old portion was left more or less intact, and when the Navy moved out in 1984

two mould lofts where full-scale plans of ships could be laid out. The smithery where iron parts for ships were fabricated dates from 1808.

The heart of the dockyard was the dry dock, and the impressive No 2 dock at Chatham dates from 1858, replacing the earlier dock where the

One of Chatham's spacious slips, covered as a protection against the weather, in which ships were built

almost all the essential features of a dockyard of the age of sail still remained. It is possible to get a vivid sense of the environment in which such ships as the *Victory*, construction of which began at Chatham in 1759, were built.

The Chatham Historic Dockyard Trust provides a visitor centre in a galvanising shop of the 1890s which is the best starting point for a tour. The dockyard comprises an ensemble of quite outstanding buildings, some remarkable for their elegance, some for their unique construction. One range was concerned with the preparation of timber for shipbuilding. There is a shed of the 1770s, built to ensure the proper seasoning of wood, sawmills of 1812—14 designed by Marc Brunel and

Victory was built. Nearby stands a range of covered building slips, the earliest of which dates from 1838 and is entirely of timber construction, while the last, of 1855, has an all-metal frame. The Colour Loft of the 1720s was where flags and sails were made. A private company still makes flags on the premises. Two vast ranges of buildings dominated the southern end of the dockyard. The Anchor Wharf storehouses of 1797—1805, the largest naval storehouses in Britain, were used for providing the supplies needed by warships on active service. The Ropery, which dates from 1786—92, is even more spectacular. Ropes for commercial use are still manufactured in this vast structure, which is 347m long and 14m wide. The entrance to the dockyard is a triumphal arch built in 1719.

DIDCOT, *Oxfordshire*

The Great Western Railway between Bristol and London, designed by Isambard Kingdom Brunel and built to the broad gauge of 2.11m/7ft 0¼in, was opened in 1841. In 1844 a branch line was opened from the main line at Didcot to Oxford. In 1852 this was extended to Birmingham, and it has ever since been part of an important route between the North, the Midlands and the south of England.

Since British Rail ceased to use steam engines in the 1960s the locomotive depot at Didcot has been the headquarters of the Great Western Society, which has the largest collection of locomotives, carriages, goods waggons and other relics of the most individual of British railway companies. Most of the locomotives exemplify Great Western practice in the 20th century but Victorian examples include Wantage Tramway No 5, sometimes called *Shannon* or *Jane*, and 0—4—0 1340 *Trojan* of 1896, and there are several 19th-century passenger carriages and freight waggons. The Horse Provender Store building near the engine shed formerly provided food for the 3,000 horses used for road transport by the Great Western.

FAVERSHAM, *Kent*

Faversham, at the head of a creek off the Swale at the point where it is bridged by the main road from London to Dover, is an ancient market town, well known for its two large breweries. In the 19th century bricks were produced in the region in large quantities for London builders, and many 'clinkers' or 'burrs' (bricks which were over-fired and fused into irregular masses) can be seen incorporated into local garden walls and rockeries.

The manufacture of explosives prospered in Faversham from about 1560 until 1934, and the marshland to the north was covered with magazines and filling plants in the early years of the 20th century. Chart Gunpowder Mills which are near Stonebridge Pond and are reached by Westbrook Walk, have been restored by the Faversham Society and are regularly open to the public. The water-powered mills date from the late 18th century and are the oldest of their kind in the world. Guidance on opening hours and on all other aspects of Faversham's history is provided by the Fleur-de-Lis Heritage Centre in Preston Street.

GWR locomotives in front of the Didcot Railway Centre's main engine shed

LONDON

London is not just the seat of government in England, the residence of the monarch and the centre of the financial system. It is, and has always been, the most important single centre of manufacturing industry in Britain.

The Science Museum in South Kensington contains many exhibits which are essential to an understanding of industry in other parts of the country. The museum houses the world's best collection of early steam engines, including a Newcomen engine, a Watt engine of 1788 and the only surviving Trevithick engine. Locomotives on display include George Stephenson's *Rocket*, while

The docks and warehouses constructed on the Isle of Dogs for the West India trade

Possibly the most famous locomotive of them all: Stephenson's Rocket, *which can be seen in the Science Museum. George Stephenson, born in Newcastle in 1781, designed* Rocket *in 1829 with the help of his son Robert. The locomotive outclassed the competition in trials organised by the Liverpool and Manchester Railway*

among the machines in the textile gallery are an original Arkwright rolling spinning frame of 1769 and a drawing frame of 1780. The galleries featuring machine tools, chemicals and bridges are similarly rich in exhibits of prime importance. The Museum of London in the Barbican covers many aspects of industrial history, although there is no section which has a specifically industrial theme.

London owes much of its prosperity to its role as a port. Until the end of the 18th century most of its trade was handled at riverside wharves, but from 1800 a system of docks was developed where ships could safely remain at any state of the tide, and where goods could be unloaded into secure warehouses or into lighters (flat-bottomed barges). The process began with the West India Docks across the isthmus of the Isle of Dogs where some of the original warehouses can be seen. St Katherine's Docks near the Tower were built by Thomas Telford in 1826—8. The complex has been redeveloped but some warehouses remain and a collection of historic vessels is kept there. The whole dockland area is being redeveloped but it seems likely that most of the wet docks and some of the original warehouses will be retained. The great warehouse complex of the East India Company at Cutler Street in the City has been converted to offices.

London is the centre of the British railway system. Its first main-line railway was the London and Greenwich, opened in 1836, which approached its terminus at London

Bridge on a 4-mile-long viaduct of 878 brick arches. This, the first great urban railway viaduct, was the forerunner of many others which were to provide accommodation for small businesses in their arches. Most of London's termini are of interest, the most spectacular being St Pancras, built in 1868-74 with a single 74m-span trainshed by W H Barlow and fronted by George Gilbert Scott's palatial hotel, Matthew Digby Wyatt's Paddington of 1855, Lewis Cubitt's elegant King's Cross of 1850—2 and Edward Wilson's vast Liverpool Street of 1872—5. Another railway building of outstanding importance is the Roundhouse at Camden, a locomotive depot of 1847.

Making London a healthy place to live in was one of the great achievements of the Victorian age. Some of the principal streets like Kingsway and High Holborn were built as part of slum clearance schemes. The Embankment was part of an ambitious scheme by Sir Joseph Bazalgette, providing a cover for a main sewer and for the District Railway. Bazalgette's Northern and Southern Outfall Sewers can be followed as footpaths in east London and Woolwich. The Northern Outfall passes Abbey Mills Pumping Station of 1869, the most spectacular in Britain. At Kew Bridge Pumping Station, the most accessible of London's temples of public health, six water pumping engines of 1820—71 are exhibited and frequently steamed.

All over central London are blocks of apartments for working people built by charitable trusts until the 1890s and then by the London County Council. The oldest surviving block, and almost the first of its kind, is now called Parnell House and stands in Streatham Street by the British Museum. It was designed by Henry Roberts and put up in 1850. Many such blocks were built by the Peabody Trust, established by an American philanthropist in 1862.

Municipal architecture with a flourish: the ornate Abbey Mills Pumping Station

MAIDENHEAD, *Berkshire*
Isambard Kingdom Brunel carried the Great Western Railway over the Thames at Maidenhead on a remarkable bridge which consists of two brick arches, some of the flattest ever constructed in brick. Each has a span of 39m with a rise of 7.4m in the centre. Many critics forecast that the arches would collapse but they safely withstood the removal of the centres, and the line was opened to traffic in 1838.

Isambard Kingdom Brunel, the Victorian engineering genius, and one of his many achievements — the railway bridge at Maidenhead, which frames Sir Robert Taylor's road bridge

In the late 19th century when the number of tracks forming the main line was increased from two to four, the bridge was widened, using the same principles of construction as those employed by Brunel. The bridge still carries an intensive service of suburban trains and expresses to the west of England and south Wales. It is best appreciated from the Thames towpath on the downstream side. Less than a mile to the east is the elegant bridge by which Brunel carried the Great Western over the old Bath Road, which itself crosses the Thames at Maidenhead on a beautiful bridge with seven water arches designed by Sir Robert Taylor and built between 1772 and 1777.

NEW RIVER, *Hertfordshire*
The New River is a 24-mile-long artificial cut which was dug in the early 17th century to provide water for London, was improved throughout the Industrial Revolution period, and is still in use. It was completed by Sir Hugh Myddelton in 1613. Much of it is still open waterway and is easy to follow. The original start of the New River was at Chadwell Spring (about 1½ miles east of Hertford), which can readily be seen from the A119 opposite the entrance to Chadwell Spring Golf Club. An inscribed monument records some of the key dates in the history of the waterway. In 1660 the River Company gained authority to take water from the River Lee and the New River Intake House where this was done can be found by walking along the towpath of the Lee Navigation from Hertford or Ware Lock. It bears an inscription recording its rebuilding in 1770.

The New River flows south through Hoddesdon, Cheshunt and Enfield — where there is an abandoned iron aqueduct of 1820 in Whitewebbs Park — to the New River Head, Islington, where several buildings relating to the company can be seen in the vicinity of Myddelton Square.

PORTSMOUTH, *Hampshire*

The Victory *stands next to the No 1 Dock Basin and 18th –century buildings*

Portsmouth's history is inextricably linked with that of the Royal Navy. It is a city rich in museums, many of them associated with the Navy. One museum with an important place in the industrial history of Portsmouth is the Eastney Pumping Station in Henderson Road, 2 miles from the town centre off the A288. Two James Watt compound rotative beam engines of 1886—7, formerly used for pumping sewage, are preserved here — and regularly steamed — together with two Crossley two-cylinder horizontally-opposed gas engines, most unusual survivals from 1904. The pumping station is in the care of the city museum service.

The prime interest of Portsmouth to the industrial archaeologist lies in the dockyard where the *Victory* and the *Mary Rose* are displayed. The docks themselves, grouped around the Great Ship Basin, are constructed of Portland Stone. The basin itself, with docks 5 and 6, dates from 1691—8, but it was greatly enlarged in 1795—1801 by Sir Samuel Bentham, who constructed docks 1, 2 and 3. HMS *Victory* reposes

in dock 2. The block mills are perhaps the most significant dockyard buildings in the history of technology for they were built in 1802 to house machinery for making rigging blocks devised by Marc Brunel, and are generally recognised as the first application of machine tools for mass production.

Boathouse No 6 or the Masthouse is of cast-iron construction, dates from 1843, and was designed to carry exceptionally heavy loads on both first and second floors. The 333m-long Great Ropery dates from 1775 and is now used for storage purposes. The No 1 Ship Shop was built in 1867 and had imposing arched entrances at each end to allow a rail track to run through it. It was extended in 1896. The 183m-long No 2 Ship Shop is in a mixture of red brick and Portland Stone and was built in 1849 for the assembly of steam engines at the time when the Navy was turning away from sail. As the working dockyard is transformed to meet the changing needs of the Royal Navy, so more and more of the historic buildings are becoming accessible to the public.

This beautifully decorated fire engine of 1862 can be seen in the Museum of London

St Pancras Station, built in the second half of the 19th century, is the most splendid monument to the Railway Age in London.

An oil painting of SS St Louis by Antonio Jacobsen, 1908, from Southampton's Maritime Museum

People are today's payload on the Ffestiniog Railway, a narrow-gauge line originally built to carry slate from Blaenau Ffestiniog to the coast

The ruins of Blaenavon ironworks, just south of the Heads of the Valleys road

Below ground at Blaenavon on a guided tour at Big Pit, an old coalmine open to the public

The lavish decor within Cardiff Castle is a reflection of the fantastic wealth generated by the city's docks during the booming 19th century

Thomas Telford, who transformed communications during the early 19th century, built this sensitively styled bridge at medieval Conwy

One of the powerful engines at the Welsh Industrial and Maritime Museum, Cardiff

The terraced streets built to house the mining communities of the steep-sided South Wales valleys

Settling ponds at the foot of Parys Mountain, where copper sludge was produced by mixing scrap iron with waste water from the copper mines

In North Wales, slate was split into almost wafer-thin tiles from huge slabs

SHEERNESS, *Kent*

Sheerness dockyard, on the Isle of Sheppey at the mouth of the Medway, was established by the Royal Navy by the 17th century. But it was in a remote spot, and in the late 18th century its buildings were supplemented by the hulks of redundant warships. It was never a popular place amongst naval personnel or civilian craftsmen, and the dockyard was relinquished by the Navy in 1960. Subsequently Sheerness has prospered as the ferry port for Vlissingen (Flushing), as the site of a modern steelworks and as a place for importing cars. One building of outstanding importance remains from the Royal Navy Dockyard, and it can easily be seen from the ferry berth. This is the Boatstore designed in 1858—60 by Colonel G T Greene, Director of Engineering and Architectural Works to the Admiralty. The Boatstore was one of the first buildings in which the load was carried by an iron frame with cast-iron uprights and fabricated wrought-iron cross girders, the outer walls being merely cladding, not load-bearing structures. As such it is rightly regarded as one of the forerunners of the modern movement in architecture.

Sheerness, now a ferry port, was once a naval dockyard

SOUTHAMPTON, *Hampshire*

Southampton was an important port in the Middle Ages but was eclipsed by other ports in the early modern period. With the coming of railways in the 19th century it enjoyed a revival, and in the 20th century became the premier passenger port in Britain until the 1950s and 60s when the ocean liner gave way to the jet aircraft. The Southampton Dock Company built the first dock in 1842, and from 1892 the port was operated by the London and

The Empress Dock, Southampton

Southampton's Empress Dock at the turn of the century

South Western Railway. The Princess Alexandra (Outer) Dock is all that now remains of the original dock installations of 1842. The Empress Dock, which was opened by Queen Victoria in 1890, has been very little changed. The Old Dock House bears the initials of the London and South Western Railway and was built in 1899, shortly after the railway company took over the docks. Most of the other installations in the docks date from the 20th century.

Southampton Pier, opened in 1833, was used for both transport and recreational purposes. Steamers for the Isle of Wight formerly started there, and it had a bandstand and tea rooms, but its future is uncertain.

The Terminus Station, 1950

Southampton Terminus Station, designed by Sir William Tite and built in 1839, is an elegant building of three storeys and five bays. It is one of the few surviving railway termini of such an early date, but all rail traffic is now concentrated at the present Southampton station and the platforms are used for car parking. Grand hotels were an important part of Victorian transport history. South Western House, now used as offices, was opened as the Imperial Hotel in 1869 and taken over by the London and South Western Railway around three years later.

Eastleigh, 6 miles north of Southampton, is one of the classic railway towns, where the London and South Western Railway established locomotive and carriage works in 1888. The company built houses for their workpeople, and of these, Dutton Cottages of 1892 still stand, together with some houses of 1899. Conegar Lock $\frac{1}{2}$ mile east of Eastleigh off the B3037 is the most complete of those remaining on the Itchen Navigation between Southampton and Winchester.

WADHURST, *East Sussex*
Wadhurst, where the B2100 crosses the B2099 some 5 miles south-east of Tunbridge Wells, lies at the heart of the Weald. In the 16th and 17th centuries this area in west Kent, east Sussex and the southern borders of Surrey was the most important iron-making region in Britain. The last Wealden iron was smelted at the furnace at Ashburnham in 1813, and the manufacture of wrought iron in the region ceased when Ashburnham forge closed about 1820. There are few surviving remains of the buildings associated with the industry, although the museums at Lewes and Hastings contain collections of such products as firebacks, as well

Firebacks were sometimes highly decorative

as material from archaeological excavations carried out in the last 20 years. Furnace Mill, Furnace Wood, Cinderhill and many other place names associated with iron-making can be identified in the area around Wadhurst, but the collection of over 30 cast-iron grave slabs in the parish church is perhaps the most impressive memorial to the vanished industry. The earliest dates from 1617 and the last from 1771 and most mark the burials of members of the Barham family.

WEALD AND DOWNLAND MUSEUM, West Sussex

The museum, a mixture of rural and industrial influences, stands in beautiful countryside

The Weald and Downland Museum at Singleton on the A286 between Chichester and Midhurst was established in 1967. Although primarily concerned with the traditional buildings and rural crafts of south-east England, many of its exhibits relate to industrial heritage. It is an open-air museum to which buildings have been moved from other parts of the region. The woodcraft area has a series of exhibits including a traditional pit for sawing by hand showing how timber was worked until the early years of the 20th century.

Charcoal burning is an important activity at the museum, and it is often possible to see in use the techniques employed by those who provided fuel for the iron furnaces of the Weald. Granaries supported on staddle stones came into widespread use in southern England during the 18th century. The museum includes one from Littlehampton which probably dates from 1731, and has a rather larger capacity than was usual. There are also smaller granaries from Goodwood and West Ashling. The Lurgashall watermill provides one of the best opportunities

in Britain to see water power in operation. It is probably of 17th century date, although most of its machinery, including its cast-iron waterwheel, was installed in the 19th century.

The museum houses a small windpump from Pevensey, typical of many erected in the region in the late 19th century, and a horse gin also of the 19th century which was used for pumping water in the village of Patching. Two important rural industries are represented by a smithy and a carpenter's shop.

One of the most interesting buildings at the museum is a turnpike toll cottage which originally stood at Upper Beeding near Shoreham. It was probably built about 1807 when parliamentary approval was given for the construction of a new line of road avoiding Beeding Hill. The cottage is of timber-framed construction and originally consisted of no more than two rooms. A toll board listing the charges to be made at turnpike gates is displayed, together with a milestone from Erringham, on the same stretch of turnpike road as that of the cottage.

WALES

*W*ales provided four raw materials — coal, iron ore, copper ore and slate — which were critical to the early stages of the Industrial Revolution. The presence of these materials transformed the areas in which they were exploited. The iron and coal of the valleys of south Wales had been worked for many centuries, but the establishment of blast furnaces along the heads of the valleys in the second half of the 18th century utterly changed the nature of the region, and within a few decades Merthyr Tydfil became the greatest centre of iron production in the world. In the late 19th century iron-making declined, but new settlements grew up in areas like the Rhondda Valley as the production of steam coal boomed.

The availability of coal was the reason for the growth of copper smelting in the Swansea Valley. Some of the copper smelted there in the late 18th century came from the great mine at Parys Mountain on Anglesey, which was visited by many tourists who found it an overpowering spectacle. The great slate quarries and mines of the Ogwen Valley, Llanberis and Blaenau Ffestiniog provided roofing materials for much of Britain as well as for many places overseas. The Welsh textile industry prospered in the 19th century, but most of its mills were of modest size and situated in rural areas or small towns.

Merthyr Tydfil's baronial Cyfarthfa Castle, built in the 1820s by the town's all-powerful ironmasters

PARYS MOUNTAIN

CONWY
HOLYWELL
LLANBERIS *HOLYHEAD ROAD* BERSHAM
BLAENAU FFESTINIOG PONTCYSYLLTE

NEWTOWN

DOLAUCOTHI
DRE-FACH FELINDRE
HEADS OF THE VALLEYS ROAD
ABERDULAIS *RHONDDA*
SWANSEA
ST FAGANS
CARDIFF

0   10   20   30 mls
0   10   20   30   40   50 kms

ABERDULAIS, *West Glamorgan*

The waterfall at Aberdulais 2 miles east of Neath on the A465 is one of the most celebrated beauty spots in Wales and has been painted by many famous artists. It has also been the scene of industrial activity for the last four centuries, its water power having been used for copper smelting, ironworking and corn milling. A weir, leats and tail races, and a wheel pit can be seen, together with a massive arched bastion which supported a trough conveying water to a waterwheel. Its last

These falls were the scene of early industrial activity

industrial use was as a tinplate works, and there are many remains from this period. Since 1981 Aberdulais Falls has been in the care of the National Trust, and it is possible to see archaeological work in progress, together with historical displays which include copies of pictures by celebrated painters.

On the south side of the A465 at Aberdulais are some important remains of the local waterways system — a canal basin, the junction of the Neath and Tennant Canals, and a 104m-long aqueduct carrying the former over the River Neath.

BERSHAM, *Clwyd*

Bersham near Wrexham was the site of one of the principal works of John Wilkinson, perhaps the best-known ironmaster of the 18th century. The Bersham Heritage Centre, in a

The elaborate roof of an octagonal building which formed part of the Bersham Ironworks

converted school at the intersection of the B5098 and B5099 just off the A483 Wrexham bypass, provides an excellent introduction, not just to the ironworking sites but to a complex industrial landscape extending for about 7 miles along the River Clywedog. An exhibition relating to John Wilkinson provides clues to the understanding of the remains of his works in the vicinity. There is also a display which features the work of the Davies Brothers, the 18th-century blacksmiths from Croes Foel, just south of Bersham, who were celebrated for their ornamental work, and made the magnificent decorative gates at nearby Chirk Castle. The centre provides leaflets describing the Bersham and Clywedog Industrial Trail, which can be followed either on foot or in a car, and links mills, lead mines, engine houses and workers' cottages between Minera and Wrexham.

BLAENAU FFESTINIOG, *Gwynedd*

Blaenau Ffestiniog was one of the world's chief sources of roofing slate in the 19th century. It is a remarkable town of stone terraces interspersed with imposing chapels and overshadowed by vast tips of slate quarry waste. Two conservation projects provide a means of learning about the quarries and those who worked in them. In the Llechwedd Slate Caverns visitors can go underground on trains through some of the 16 levels of one of the largest slate mines in Wales. The Llechwedd site is notable for its railway inclined planes, and there is a museum of slate working on the surface. It is also possible to go underground at Gloddfa Ganol, where the displays include some slateworkers' houses.

Blaenau Ffestiniog is as famous for the means by which slate was conveyed to the coast as it is for its quarrying. The Ffestiniog Railway was opened in 1836 to convey slate to Porthmadog. There was a fall of some 210m/700ft in the 13 miles from Blaenau Ffestiniog to the coast.

Originally, loaded waggons descended by gravity, while horses were used to pull the empties back up the hill. In 1865 the line was rebuilt to be worked by the steam locomotives of 0.59m/1ft 11½in gauge. A passenger service was operated and the railway became famous for its double-ended locomotives designed by Robert Francis Fairlie.

During the 20th century the line lost traffic, and was closed for a time before being revived by a preservation society in the early 1950s. Starting with a short length of track near Porthmadog, the company gradually brought more and more of the railway back into commission, and it is now possible to travel across curving drystone viaducts and along shelves cut from mountainsides all the way from the quay at Porthmadog to Blaenau Ffestiniog.

Near Tan-y-Bwlch station the line crosses a road on an iron bridge cast at the company's foundry at Boston Lodge in 1854. Locomotives used on the line include several of the original double-ended Fairlies.

Slate was transported by rail from Blaenau Ffestiniog to Porthmadog for shipment

CARDIFF, *South Glamorgan*

Cardiff rose to prominence during the 19th century as a port from which iron and coal produced in the south Wales valleys were shipped to customers all over the world. The Glamorganshire Canal linking Cardiff with the ironworks at Merthyr Tydfil was opened in 1794, and a sea lock, enabling coastal vessels to be loaded in the basin at its terminus, was constructed four years later. In 1830 the Marquis of Bute gained authority to build the Bute West Dock, which was

Cardiff's Bute Docks in the busy 1920s

completed the following year. Other docks followed, and Cardiff was linked by many railways to the collieries in the valleys:

The Welsh Industrial and Maritime Museum has been built close to what remains of the Bute West Dock in Bute Street. Exhibits include a variety of engines used for pumping, winding and driving machines, and a working full-scale replica of Trevithick's locomotive of 1804, which ran down the Taff Valley from Merthyr Tydfil. The museum also has a railway gallery and maritime gallery, and is well located for viewing what remains of the city's docks.

CONWY, *Gwynedd*

Conwy is a small walled town, laid out in the Middle Ages around the great castle built by Edward I to guard the crossing of the estuary of the River Conwy. Until 1826 travellers along the north Wales coast had to cross the estuary by means of a ferry, but in that year Thomas Telford completed a suspension bridge, which was a smaller version of his bridge over the Menai Straits.

In 1849 Robert Stephenson carried the Chester and Holyhead Railway over the river, and he also chose a bridge built on the same principles as the one he had used to cross the Menai Straits — in this case a wrought-iron tubular bridge. Both the bridges at Conwy survive in almost unaltered form. The railway bridge is still open to traffic, while the suspension bridge has been preserved since 1965 by the National Trust and is open to pedestrians. The suspension chains are supported by pairs of stone turrets, designed to harmonise with the castle. The tollhouse at the eastern end, which serves as an information centre, is an extraordinary architectural confection in the Gothic style.

An intriguing mixture of medieval and mock military. Telford's turreted suspension bridge across the mouth of the Conwy blends in well with the town's ancient castle walls

DOLAUCOTHI, *Dyfed*

The Dolaucothi Gold Mines at Pumpsaint, east of the A482 7 miles south-east of Lampeter, were worked by the Romans soon after their arrival in Britain. Excavations have revealed remains of a fort which was built about AD75 to protect the workings. A hoard of Roman jewellery was discovered in a

Dolaucothi, the only site in Britain where the Romans definitely mined for gold

field near the mines in the 18th century. Modern mining development began at Dolaucothi in 1888 and working continued spasmodically, without any outstanding success, until 1938. Dolaucothi is in the care of the National Trust and in the summer season there are tours of the underground workings of both the Roman and modern periods. The National Trust publishes trail guides which enable visitors to discover for themselves the great variety of remains on the suface, which include traces of tramways, aqueducts and mills for crushing ore as well as entrances to adits, and traces of 'hushing' (the process by which topsoil was washed away to reveal veins of minerals). Finds from archaeological excavations at Dolaucothi are displayed in the museum at Carmarthen.

DRE-FACH FELINDRE, *Dyfed*

The manufacture of woollen textiles flourished in several parts of rural Wales in the 19th century. One of the most active textile areas was the Teifi Valley in Dyfed, where the Museum of the Welsh Woollen Industry is operated as part of the National Museum of Wales. The museum is sited in a mill at Dre-fach Felindre, about 2 miles south of Henllan which is on the A484 from Newcastle Emlyn to Carmarthen. The mill is typical of those which operated

Traditionally patterned Welsh cloth is still produced at Dre-fach Felindre

in rural Wales, and the atmosphere of a working factory has been sensitively preserved. The building has undergone few structural alterations, and some cloth is still produced here. There are displays illustrating the history of woollen cloth manufacture in Wales since the Middle Ages, and a collection of textile machinery includes some spinning jennies. A trail has been devised beginning at Dre-fach Felindre which guides visitors past several other mills and a terrace of weavers' cottages. Several mills in the vicinity are still in commercial production.

HEADS OF THE VALLEYS ROAD

The A465 across the heads of the south Wales valleys was built in the 1960s. The road can be used as a link between places which together provide a splendid introduction to the history of the iron and coal trades of south Wales.

At Blaenavon, reached by the B4246 from Abergavenny or the B4248 from Brynmawr, the remains of the ironworks are administered by the Torfaen Museum Trust. There are remains of five blast furnaces, casting houses, a water balance tower (by which waggons were raised to the level of the furnace tops) and terraces of workers' cottages. Nearby is the Big Pit Mining Museum with exhibits about mining and the life of colliery communities. There are opportunities here to go underground into the workings on guided tours.

Visitors to Big Pit descend 300ft to explore the underground workings

In the Clydach Gorge, the spectacular section of the A465 between Abergavenny and Brynmawr, the remains of the Clydach ironworks are being conserved by the district council. They can be approached along Station Road, Clydach. Alongside the Clydach ironworks is an iron tramway bridge of 1824 in the Gothic style.

Merthyr Tydfil had the greatest concentration of ironworks in the world in the early 19th century. At Dowlais on the eastern side of the town a vast brick blowing engine house remains together with the company stables. There is little left of the Cyfarthfa works to the west, but Cyfarthfa Castle, built by the owner, William Crawshay II in 1825, now houses a museum. Behind the

Merthyr Tydfil was once the 'iron-producing capital of the world'. The past is remembered at a museum within Cyfarthfa Castle, a symbol of the wealth created by the town's ironworks

Technical College can be found the bases of the Ynysfach blast furnaces and the grey-stoned shell of a blowing engine house.

There are remains of further furnaces at Hirwaun, approached by an old tramway north of the town centre. A short distance up the A4109 which joins the A465 near Aberdulais is the Cefn Coed Mining Museum, where a steam winding engine is preserved with its boilers. At Neath Abbey two blast furnaces of 1789, probably the best preserved of their type in Britain, have been acquired by the local authority, and may soon be accessible.

HOLYHEAD ROAD

Under the direction of Thomas Telford, the road between London and Holyhead was improved between 1815 and 1826 until it became the best in Europe of its date. The improvements were carried out with government money, largely because Irish MPs had to travel to Parliament in London after 1800. From Shrewsbury to Holyhead, a distance of 105 miles, the present A5 follows the line of the Holyhead Road, except on some stretches like the Oswestry bypass where recent improvements have been carried out. Milestones of a standard pattern were installed in 1828, and most of the toll cottages were rebuilt to standard designs. The first milestone can be found at the junction of The Mount and Hafren Road in Shrewsbury, and most of the remainder are still *in situ*. A toll cottage of the standard design can be found on the old route through Oswestry just beyond the town's cattle market.

One of the biggest improvements on the road was the new route from Chirk bridge to Chirk, completed in 1824, replacing a maze of old roads which ran through a muddy morass to the east of the present road. West of Chirk it is possible to observe 'depots', small recesses at the sides of the road where small stones for dressing the road surface were stored. There are further tollhouses at Llangollen and Ty-isa. After passing Corwen the road climbs the pass of Glyn Diffrwys. A farmstead at Cerniog was once the Prince Llewellyn, an important coaching inn.

At Betws-y-Coed the road crosses the Conwy on an iron bridge which an inscription proclaims was built in 1815, the year of the Battle of Waterloo. It was not actually erected until the following year but the motifs of the rose, the shamrock, the thistle and the leek in cast iron justify a close examination. After passing through Snowdonia, along the shores of Llyn Ogwen and down the pass of Nant Ffrancon, the road reaches Bangor before crossing the Menai Straits by Telford's masterpiece, the Menai Suspension Bridge, completed in 1826. Beyond the bridge, Telford's new road across Anglesey is distinguished by tollhouses with octagonal towers, and finally approaches Holyhead by the Stanley Embankment.

Telford's elegant Menai Suspension Bridge, which links Anglesey to mainland north Wales

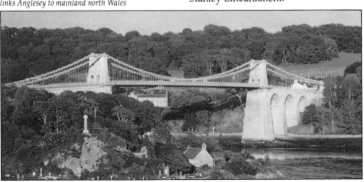

HOLYWELL, *Clwyd*

The Greenfield Valley extends about a mile and a half from the town of Holywell through a wooded valley to the A548 and the River Dee. The flow of water was once much greater than it is now, and it was believed to have miraculous properties. It can first be seen at the pilgrimage church of St Winifrede at the top of the valley. The area below came to have one of the greatest concentrations of manufacturing activity in Britain in the second half of the 18th century. The water power was used to produce copper sheathing for ships, and the copper bolts which held it in place, from ingots which had been smelted in the St Helens area from ore mined on Parys Mountain. There were also two cotton mills in the valley, modelled on those built by Richard Arkwright in Derbyshire. Later, in Victorian times, a steeply graded railway line ran through the valley linking Holywell with Holywell Junction on the line from Chester to Rhyl. The Greenfield Valley Heritage Park Visitor Centre provides an introduction to the pools, the remains of the mills and other relics of industry in the valley.

LLANBERIS, *Gwynedd*

The Dinorwic Quarry, on the north-east side of the A4086 through the pass of Llanberis, was one of the principal sources of slate in Britain. The workshops complex of the quarry now forms a museum where displays show the various skills of the quarrymen, how slate was cut, how it was shaped for the customer, and how the machinery and tools necessary for the operation of the quarry were properly maintained.

The workshops were powered by this massive waterwheel at the Welsh Slate Museum, Llanberis

It is possible to explore the four-hearth smithy, the foundry with its cupola furnace and an extensive pattern-makers' loft, and the canteen where the workers took refreshment. The restored and working waterwheel which once provided power to operate the machines was the largest in Wales. Alongside the slate museum is the terminus of the Llanberis Lake Railway on which steam locomotives draw visitors along the pleasant shores of Llyn Padarn. On the opposite side of the A4086 stand the terminus and locomotive shed of the Snowdon Mountain Railway, the only railway in Britain to use a rack system in which a cogged wheel on the locomotive interlocks with a toothed rail. It opened in 1896 and is worked by seven steam-driven and two diesel-powered narrow-gauge locomotives.

NEWTOWN, *Powys*

In the 16th and 17th centuries, and for much of the 18th, cloth-making in mid Wales was a widely scattered industry with its commercial centre over the border in Shrewsbury. In the 1780s and 90s Welsh cloth makers began to concentrate on the production of flannel, and the centre of the trade moved to the market towns of the upper Severn Valley. Welshpool and Llanidloes grew considerably at this time, but it was Newtown which was the boom town of the early 19th century, with the construction of many new houses, mills and chapels. The Newtown Textile Museum is situated in Commercial Street, and its displays include hand looms and other items relating to the flannel trade.

Newtown was known as the 'Leeds of Wales' during its cloth-producing heyday

The great social reformer Robert Owen, best known for his work at New Lanark (page 111), was born in Newtown in 1771 and died there in 1858. A memorial museum in Broad Street tells the story of his life. Pryce Jones's Royal Welsh Warehouse established in 1859 was a pioneering mail-order company and happily still flourishes.

PARYS MOUNTAIN, *Gwynedd*

Parys Mountain on Anglesey was for several decades one of the world's most important sources of copper ore. Its modern industrial history began with the discovery of ore in 1764. It was worked by two different companies, although both were controlled from 1785 by the Anglesey solicitor Thomas Williams, the 'copper king'. Ore was extracted both by mining and by blasting it from the side of the great open cast on top of the hill. Much of it was roasted to remove

Remnants of kilns on Parys Mountain

impurities in rectangular kilns, of which remains can still be seen.

Parys Mountain became one of the most visited industrial sites in Britain during the 1790s and early 1800s. Parts of the workings are dangerous, but a public footpath leading across the mountain from the B5111 provides a safe view of the great pit, notable for the almost complete absence of vegetation, which is due to the sulphur compounds in the rock. On the north side of the mountain between the B5111 and the A5025 are pits where scrap iron was placed with water from the workings. The iron dissolved leaving a copper-bearing sludge. Nearby Amlwch was the port to which the copper ore was taken for shipment.

PONTCYSYLLTE, *Clwyd*

The Pontcysyllte Aqueduct, an amazing waterway in the sky 305m long and 39m high, is one of the wonders of Wales. It was built by the Ellesmere Canal Company, an ambitious concern

Telford's magnificent Pontcysyllte Aqueduct became one of the 19th-century 'wonders of Wales'

which hoped, by uniting the Mersey, the Dee and the Severn, to provide an inland waterway linking Liverpool with Bristol. Construction of the crossing of the Dee at Pontcysyllte began in 1795, a fact recorded on a plaque at the foot of one of the highest piers, but little work was done until 1801 when the crossing of the Ceiriog at Chirk was completed.

Thomas Telford was responsible for the building of the structure, which was first crossed by boats in 1805. The ironwork was supplied by Williams Hazeldine's foundry at Plas Kynaston, on the site nearby now occupied by the Monsanto chemical works. The most interesting features can be explored from Trevor Basin at the northern end, best approached from the A539, where it is possible to see dry docks and the remains of tramways which brought coal from local collieries to be loaded on barges. The main line of the canal was never completed and the aqueduct never fulfilled its original purpose.

RHONDDA, *Mid Glamorgan*

The Rhondda is the most famous of the coal-mining valleys of south Wales, the scene of many tragedies, as well as the source of vast mineral wealth. A tour should begin at Pontypridd where the remarkable masonry bridge built by William Edward in 1755 can be seen in the town centre. The bridge stands next to an imposing chapel, which has been converted into a Historical and Cultural Centre with displays relating to Pontypridd in the industrial heyday. The A4225 passes a winding house with an engine of 1875 at Hetty Shaft, Hopkinstown, and the junction of the Rhondda Fach (the 'little' Rhondda) and the Rhondda Fawr (the 'big' Rhondda) at Porth. All through the Rhondda, curving terraces of stone houses with brick dressings face inwards across the valley, looking down on the river, the road and the railway, along which can be seen the ruins of many pits sunk during the steam coal boom of the late 19th century but now abandoned. One of the best views across the valley is seen from the B4223 at Ton Pentre on the western side. At the head of the valley beyond Treorchy and Treherbert, the A4061 quickly passes into open mountain country, and there is a superb viewpoint looking down on the head of the valley at Blaenrhondda near the S-bend high on the slopes above the reservoir.

ST FAGANS, *South Glamorgan*

The Welsh Folk Museum at St Fagans west of Cardiff, opened in 1947, was the first major open-air museum on the Scandinavian model in Britain. Buildings from all over Wales have been removed to St Fagans and re-erected, and the main museum building houses superb displays of tools, household utensils and furniture. Many of the buildings are from rural areas of Wales, but several are important parts of the Welsh industrial heritage.

Demonstrations of old skills are a regular feature at the Welsh Folk Museum

A tollhouse from outside Aberystwyth provides fascinating evidence of the workings of turnpike roads. A tannery from Rhayader was the last in Wales to use oak bark in the processing of leather. It is the best reminder in Britain of an industry which was once represented in almost every town. At the Esgair Moel woollen factory from Llanwrtyd in Powys it is possible to see woollen cloth being woven, and completed pieces are often hung on the tenter frames outside. The industrial region of south Wales is represented by a terrace of ironworkers' cottages from Merthyr Tydfil. St Fagans Castle forms part of the museum, and craftsmen, including a woodturner and a cooper, practise their trades in the outbuildings.

SWANSEA, *West Glamorgan*

Swansea, at the mouth of the River Tawe, became the chief centre for smelting Cornish copper during the 18th century, and with the building of canals and railways developed into a major coal port. The landscape of the lower Swansea Valley in the early 19th century was one of the most heavily polluted in the world, and drew expressions of horror from visitors. In recent decades the area has been the subject of reclamation schemes and much of the landscape of the copper-smelting era has disappeared.

The Maritime and Industrial Museum in a converted warehouse at the side of the South Dock provides an introduction to the history of the region. Its exhibits include the lightship *Helwick* and the steam tug *Canning*, together with a cab from a tramcar which worked on the Swansea and Mumbles Railway, the world's first passenger railway, opened in 1807. The Swansea Museum in the Royal Institution of Wales in Victoria Road has a large collection of the pottery and porcelain produced in Swansea between the 1760s and the 1860s, as well as displays relating to the landscape of the lower Swansea Valley.

Swansea ware was much sought after in the 19th century

CENTRAL ENGLAND AND EAST ANGLIA

The Black Country's blighted landscape, 1869

*T*his region includes some of the most celebrated heartlands of the Industrial Revolution. It witnessed Richard Arkwright's enterprises in the Derwent Valley in Derbyshire, Birmingham's role as the metropolis of the hardware district of the Black Country, and Coalbrookdale's pioneering work as the birthplace of the modern iron industry. In addition, the hosiery trades of Nottingham and Leicester, the engineering works of Coventry and Derby, and coalfields which extend over much of the Midlands are all known and recognised as being amongst the most important of British industries.

Yet the Industrial Revolution amounted to much more than the sudden growth of successful enterprises in a few places. The region also illustrates how new ways of living and working spread across Britain. Places like Shardlow and Stourport are magnificent reminders of the importance of the narrow canal system which provided cheap fuel in many parts of the country which had previously lacked it, as well as a means of delivering small consignments of goods reliably and quickly. East Anglia is particularly notable for the iron foundries which grew up in the early 19th century in almost every market town (in places like Ipswich, and particularly the great 'cathedral' for building traction engines at Leiston — see page 77). Few remain in use but buildings show how the principles of mechanical engineering spread across Britain.

BEWDLEY AND THE SEVERN VALLEY RAILWAY, *Hereford and Worcester/Shropshire*

The Severn Valley Railway fom Shrewsbury to Hartlebury was opened in 1862. After its closure in the 1960s, the section south of Bridgnorth was rescued by enthusiasts and is now one of Britain's leading preserved railways, with a 16-mile line from Bridgnorth to Kidderminster, and a superb collection of rolling stock, the largest in the

and a glass blower. It also includes notable displays on rope-making and on the industries of the Wyre Forest, including charcoal-burning and basket-making, and there is also a working timber yard. On the quayside are several flights of steps which gave access to barges moored on the river, while there is a roller above the towpath arch of the bridge which protected the stonework from the ropes used to haul vessels going upstream.

An ex-British Rail 'Standard' Class 4 locomotive steaming along the line

country. Bridgnorth was once a river port to which waggons and packhorses brought goods from as far away as Manchester and the Potteries. There are still warehouse buildings in Low Town, the riverside portion of the town. The town centre on top of a hill can be reached from the riverside by Britain's only inland cliff railway, or by The Cartway, a twisting street of tiny cottages once occupied by bargemen and carpet weavers.

Bewdley has a splendid river frontage on either side of the stone bridge constructed by Thomas Telford in the 1790s. The museum in the old butchers' shambles occasionally has displays by working craftsmen, including a pewterer, a brass founder

The railway and the river towpath between Arley and Eardington give access to a landscape rich in remains of collieries, sandstone quarries and iron forges, as well as the magnificent cast-iron Victoria Bridge which takes the railway over the Severn. It was designed by John Fowler, 20 years later the designer of the Forth Bridge, and the castings were made by the Coalbrookdale Company. It can be seen by following the river towpath downstream from Arley. An iron bridge of 1828, also cast by the Coalbrookdale Company, carries the towpath over the mouth of the Borle Brook downstream from Highley, while another cast by Onions and Co of Broseley crosses the Mor Brook near Eardington.

Beer delivery vehicles of old at the Bass Museum of Brewing History, Burton upon Trent

One of the exhibits at the National Tramway Museum, Crich

Lead was once extracted in great quantities from Derbyshire's Magpie Mine

Above and right: *Ironware and beautiful porcelain, some of the extensive range of products on view in the museums of the Ironbridge Gorge*

Printing skills preserved at Blists Hill, part of the Ironbridge museums complex

North Street, Cromford, built in about 1777 by Richard Arkwright for his cotton mill workers

Above: This 'miner's hovel' can be seen at the Black Country Museum, Dudley

Left: Another worker's dwelling — this time a chain-maker's cottage — at the Black Country Museum

The High-Level Bridge across the Tyne at Newcastle

An old tram, period shops and street scenes help re-create a bygone way of life at the North of England Open-Air Museum, Beamish

BIRMINGHAM, *West Midlands*

Birmingham was one of the fastest-growing cities of the Industrial Revolution, one of the most important metal-working centres in the world, and the scene of numerous important innovations. It was traditionally a city of workshops and the atmosphere of small-scale Victorian enterprise can be experienced in the restored Jewellery Quarter around the Church of St Paul, Hockley, north-west of the centre.

Birmingham became the nodal point of the Midlands canal system following the opening of the Birmingham Canal linking the city with the collieries of the Black Country in 1768. A network of canals remains, largely hidden, in the city centre. It is accessible from the walkway past Farmer's Bridge locks.

Birmingham is the centre of the national railway system, but the most interesting monuments of railway history in the city are to the south of the centre away from the modern New Street Station. Philip Hardwick's Curzon Street Station, opened in 1838, was the original terminus of the London and Birmingham Railway.

Its classical style matched that of the original Euston Station at the other end of the line. The station building is now used as offices. Nearby are the remains of the Duddeston Viaduct, built to link the lines from Coventry and Leamington in the 1840s but never actually used. Many of its arches are now workshops. A good view can be obtained from Sandy Lane. Steam locomotives are maintained within the Birmingham Railway Museum at Tyseley.

The Birmingham Museum of Science and Industry in Newhall Street is situated in an old electro-plating factory above the Birmingham and Fazeley Canal. It has a large collection of exhibits relating to the city's industrial past, including the steam engine built by Boulton and Watt on the Birmingham Canal at Smethwick in 1779, and the ingenious letter copying machines designed by James Watt. Many of the smaller items produced in the city — buttons, plated wares and the like — can be seen in the Museum and Art Gallery in Chamberlain Square. Sarehole Mill, in Colebank Road, Hall Green, which is maintained

The Museum of Science and Industry's Engineering Hall

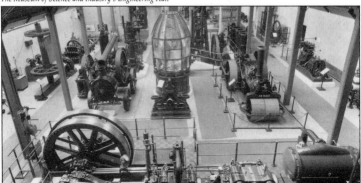

by the city museums service, is a corn mill, on a site once used by Matthew Boulton as a slitting mill for iron. Water power was one of the foundations of Birmingham's prosperity in the 18th century when there were more than 50 mills within the present bounds of the city.

Birmingham's industrial history in the second half of the 18th century was dominated by Matthew Boulton and James Watt, builders of steam engines and innovators in many spheres. Their Soho Manufactory, built in 1762, was demolished in the 1860s, but Soho Foundry, opened in 1796, remains in industrial use. Their memorials, together with one commemorating William Murdock, pioneer of gas lighting, can be seen in St Mary's Church, Handsworth.

Bournville, 4 miles south of the centre, was built from 1894 onwards by George Cadbury, around the chocolate and cocoa factory to which he and Richard Cadbury had moved their business from the city centre in 1879.

Bournville cocoa being packed, 1925

Cadbury employed the architect W Alexander Harvey to create a garden suburb of carefully designed houses set in large gardens, with a generous provision of schools, shops and places of worship, and even a pair of old timber-framed buildings from the Warwickshire countryside. It was always intended that Bournville should not be restricted to employees at the chocolate factory. George Cadbury was a Quaker who hoped that the example which he set at Bournville would be followed elsewhere, and in many respects his achievements have been so influential that the streets of Bournville seem quite commonplace. When they

George Cadbury, a member of a family that became a household name

are compared with the neighbouring areas of late Victorian and Edwardian Birmingham it becomes clear how much of a novelty they were at the time they were built.

BURTON UPON TRENT,
Staffordshire

Burton upon Trent has been the most important single centre of the brewing industry in Britain since the 18th century, and the town is still dominated by the massive plants of the principal brewing companies. The industry has been transformed since World War II, and many traditional breweries and maltings have been demolished and replaced by modern structures. Marston's Albion Brewery of 1875 is the outstanding survivor from the 19th century.

Delivering the barrels the traditional way outside the Bass Museum

The best starting point for a visit to Burton is the Bass Museum of Brewing History in Horninglow Street just north of the town centre, which is housed in a three-storey building which once accommodated the joiners' shops of a brewery. Exhibits include a steam engine, a complete model of a brewery and one of the tank locomotives which formerly shunted waggons around the sharp curves of the railway system which ran through the streets of the town linking the principal breweries and maltings. The Arkwright Society publishes a guide to Burton available at local museums and shops which identifies the surviving buildings of two cotton mills built by Sir Robert Peel.

COVENTRY, *West Midlands*

In recent times Coventry has been famous for making motor cars, motorcycles and tractors, but its industrial history stretches back many centuries. By the early 18th century the city was celebrated for making ribbons and tapes, and the name tapes used by many schoolchildren to identify their clothes are still made in Coventry. The ribbon industry underwent something of a revolution in the early 19th century and in Cash's Lane, Coventry there stands a remarkable terrace of forty 3-storey half-timbered cottages, built by J and J Cash about 1840 for their ribbon weavers. It was one of several such 'cottage factories' built in Coventry at that time. In the 18th and

Mass production — another industrial milestone — at a Coventry car factory

19th centuries Coventry was also famous for its watches, and several watchmakers' workshops survive in the Chapelfields area. The Singer works in Canterbury Street was built about 1880 for the manufacture of sewing machines, but was later used for making motor cars. The Herbert Art Gallery and Museum has Jacquard looms and other exhibits illustrating Coventry's old industries as well as its 20th-century manufactures.

CRICH, *Derbyshire*

The electric tramcar — the 'gondola of the people' — began to replace the earlier horse, cable and steam trams in the principal cities of Britain in the 1880s. Crich, 2 miles east of the A6 on the B5035, is the home of the country's largest collection of tramcars. The collection is located in an old limestone quarry, and it is possible to travel on a mile-long track in a great assortment of vehicles. The façade of the Assembly

The front of Derby's impressive Assembly Room has been moved to Crich

Room from Derby, built in 1763—4, has been re-erected at the museum, together with a bandstand from Manchester, and various items of 19th-century street furniture. The museum's collection of tramcars amounts to more than 50 vehicles. Nineteenth-century examples include a horse tram built in Birkenhead in 1873 for export to Portugal and a steam tram locomotive built by the famous Manchester firm of Beyer Peacock in 1885 for use in Australia. The majority of the tramcars at Crich, however, date from the 20th century and draw their power from overhead wires.

CROMFORD, *Derbyshire*

Cromford is an entrancing *mélange* of running water and hard, grey stone, one of the most evocative of all monuments of the Industrial Revolution in Britain. Richard Arkwright, whose water frame transformed the cotton industry, built a five-storey water-powered mill in Cromford in 1771. The original mill still stands but it was reduced from five storeys to three by a fire in 1929. It is located at one end of a complex of mills and warehouses which grew up within 20 years after 1771. The mills are being restored by the Arkwright Society who have a visitor centre and shop within the complex.

North of Cromford village on the A6 is Masson Mill which Arkwright built in 1784—5, by which time he had become highly successful. Its elegant brick frontage with its Venetian windows and cupola are in marked contrast to the gaunt brick of the original mill complex.

Cromford's Masson Mill. The date 1769 on the building refers to Arkwright's first factory in Nottingham, where the machines were worked by horse power

Around his mills Arkwright built a village to house his workpeople. The three-storey cottages in North Street, which have 'weavers' windows' with long lights on the top floors, were built in 1777, probably to attract male weavers (or knitters) who worked at home while their wives and children were employed at spinning in the mills. Later terraces do not have such

Cromford's market place grew up around Richard Arkwright's pioneering cotton mill

windows. Arkwright laid out the market place, and built the Greyhound Hotel, known as the Black Dog in the 18th century, and the parish church near the River Derwent. His descendants built the village school in North Street in 1832. At the centre of Cromford is a reservoir, in which the waters of the Bonsall Brook were stored before being used to power the waterwheels of the cotton mills. At the upper end of the pool, the corn mill built by Arkwright to supply the village is being restored by the Arkwright Society, who publish a useful trail guide to Cromford and its surroundings.

DERBY, *Derbyshire*

Britain's first textile factory was built at Derby around 1717. It was a silk-throwing mill of five storeys, using Italian technology, and constructed by Thomas Lombe. The building became

A harbinger of a new age: Britain's earliest textile factory

famous and drew many visitors in the 18th century. It was destroyed in a fire in 1910, and then rebuilt to the same dimensions but with three storeys. It now contains Derby's Industrial Museum which has a major collection of Rolls-Royce aero engines and will shortly house a splendid model displaying the Midland Railway of which Derby was the hub. Several terraces of workers' houses of the 1840s built by the company have been restored near the station. Two miles north of the city centre is Darley Abbey where Thomas Evans, an associate of Richard Arkwright, established a cotton factory from 1783. The mill buildings are now used for other purposes, but most of the village built by the Evans family remains. There are elegant three-storey terraces of workers' cottages, 'cluster houses' built in blocks of four which accommodated foremen and other senior workpeople, and an elegant school of 1826. Memorials to the Evans family can be seen in the local parish church.

DUDLEY, *West Midlands*

Dudley is built around its castle on the summit of the ridge which divides in two the area which has long been known as the Black Country, one of the greatest concentrations of heavy industry in Britain. In the 17th century much of this area was open heathland, on which smiths making nails, locks, chains and edge tools built cottages and workshops. From the end of the 18th century the Black Country was one of the world's leading sources of iron. Iron-making declined at the end of the 19th century as local supplies of ore and coal ran out, but the rolling, forging, and casting of iron and steel continued, and in spite of recent setbacks, many works still flourish.

The Black Country Museum off the Birmingham—Wolverhampton A4123 'New Road' is the best introduction to the area's industrial and social history. Buildings which have been moved to the museum include a pub and a Methodist chapel. From time to time it is possible to see steel rolled in the museum's rolling mill. The museum houses a replica of a Newcomen engine. It is also the starting point for boat trips through the canal tunnel which goes under the limestone ridge to the west, and passes through spectacular caverns where limestone was mined.

Mushroom Green (now a conservation area) is a collection of cottages and workshops typical of those which grew up on the heathlands of the Black Country. It is situated north of Cradley Heath, and is approached along St Anne's Road and Quarry Road. The buildings include a chainmaker's shop in which demonstrations are organised by the Black Country Museum.

The Dudley area is intersected by a dense network of canals which were one of the foundations of its industrial prosperity in the 18th and 19th centuries. One of the most impressive features is the flight of eight locks (originally nine) at Delph on the Dudley Canal, best approached from Delph Road which links the A459 and the A4100 south of Brierley Hill.

Visitors to Dudley can take canal boat trips through tunnels and caverns

IRONBRIDGE, *Shropshire*

The bridge that has become the symbol of Britain's Industrial Revolution

The Ironbridge Gorge where the River Severn cuts through the Shropshire coalfield was the most important iron-making area in the world in the late 18th century, when glowing furnaces, creaking steam engines and billowing clouds of smoke of many colours could be seen in a magnificent natural setting. The area was celebrated for its innovations: the first iron rails, the first iron boat, the first steam railway locomotive; above all for the symbol of its success, the famous Iron Bridge constructed in the summer of 1779 and opened on New Year's Day 1781. The area's industry stagnated in the first half of the 19th century and rapidly declined in the second, but since the 1960s the many monuments of the Industrial Revolution in the gorge have been restored by the Ironbridge Gorge Museum Trust. In 1987 the Ironbridge Gorge was amongst the first places in Britain to be designated a UNESCO World Heritage Site.

The Iron Bridge is the centrepiece of the gorge. It has been closed to motor traffic since 1934 but visitors can cross it on foot and go underneath to examine the principles of construction. The Museum Trust has an information centre in the tollhouse on the bridge with displays illustrating its history, and about 400m away is the Museum Visitor Centre in a riverside warehouse built in Gothic style.

Coalbrookdale, a mile from the bridge, has been an ironworking community for four centuries. It was here in 1709 that the first of four ironmasters to bear the name Abraham Darby succeeded in smelting iron using coke rather than charcoal as his fuel. The water-powered furnace where

Darby smelted his iron ceased operation in 1818, but it still stands, protected by a modern cover building erected by the Museum Trust in 1982. Alongside is the Museum of Iron, a rich treasure chest of iron products, with illustrations of iron-making processes through the centuries.

Iron being poured into moulds in the foundry at Blists Hill, Ironbridge

Between the furnace and the Museum of Iron is a gallery where exhibitions from the magnificent collection of paintings of industrial scenes assembled by the late Sir Arthur Elton are displayed. A short distance away is Rosehill House, which the Museum Trust has refurnished to show something of the way of life of the 19th-century ironmaster's family.

About 2 miles from the Iron Bridge is the Blists Hill Open-Air Museum which portrays life in an industrial community of about a century ago. At the top of Blists Hill is a town area, made up of buildings which have been brought in from elsewhere, including a printing shop, a candlemaker's, and a bank where shillings and pence to make purchases in the shops can be obtained. A steam engine winds a cage in and out of a mine, and there is a foundry where molten iron is cast once a week. At the foot of the hill are the ruins of three 19th-century blast furnaces, and a re-erected works where wrought iron is occasionally made in puddling furnaces, shingled (pounded to remove impurities) under a steam hammer and rolled in a rolling mill. Beyond the ironworks is a woodland area which culminates in the spectacular Hay Inclined Plane, by which canal boats were lifted up and down the side of the gorge.

The Coalport China Museum stands on the north bank of the Severn

The Coalport China Works, part of the Ironbridge Gorge museum complex

2 miles from the Iron Bridge. Porcelain was made at Coalport from the 1790s until 1926. The museum includes a brilliant display of wares in one of the bottle ovens. Nearby it is possible to go underground in the 200-year-old Tar Tunnel and see natural bitumen oozing from the sides. On the opposite bank of the Severn is the Jackfield Tile Museum, where the tiles which lit up late 19th- and early 20th-century homes and public buildings with vivid colours are displayed within a former tile factory.

LEISTON, *Suffolk*

The making of iron castings is one of the foundations of the modern engineering industry. It was a technique which spread in the early part of the 19th century from the big cities and the traditional iron-making regions like Shropshire and the Weald to almost every market town of any standing in England. Most ironfounders in such towns were engaged in the manufacture of agricultural machinery.

East Anglia, the leading arable farming region in Britain, was well-supplied with foundries by 1850, some of which were exporting such products as reapers, threshing machines and steam engines to many parts of the world. From the 1870s, corn farmers faced increasing difficulties and many East Anglian foundries turned to making their livings from other products such as tortoise stoves, mining machinery and piano frames. One of the best-known firms in the region was Garretts of Leiston, established in 1778 as a blacksmithing business. The company's Long Shop, otherwise known as 'the cathedral', was built in 1853 as an erecting shop for traction engines. This spectacular building is now preserved as a fascinating museum.

Inside the Long Shop

MAGPIE MINE, *Derbyshire*

The Peak District in Derbyshire was one of the most important sources of lead in Britain in the 18th century. Some sites were developed on a large scale in the early 19th century, with steam pumping engines and extensive dressing floors, but the industry declined rapidly after 1860.

The Peak District Mining Museum in Matlock Bath on the A6 provides an introduction to the subject, but the most dramatic site to visit is Magpie Mine, a prominent local landmark. This can either be approached by a footpath

Engine houses and other buildings around the top of the shaft at Magpie Mine

from the village of Sheldon about a mile west of the A6 at Ashford, or by car along a minor road which forks right off the B5055 west of Bakewell and then maintains a roughly parallel course to Monyash. Magpie Mine was a rich source of lead for more than two centuries. The remains include an engine house of 1869—70, a chimney of 1840, one old and one modern winding house, an agent's cottage and a power house. Unfilled shafts make the area hazardous for the unwary, but it is possible to examine the principal structures in complete safety. The Peak District Mines Historical Society now administers the site.

NORWICH, *Norfolk*

Norwich in the early 18th century was one of the great centres of the English woollen cloth trade. Manufacture, on a domestic basis, was spread throughout the surrounding countryside. The city's textile industry declined at the end of the 18th century, although there were attempts to sustain it by constructing factories. In 1839 a handsome mill with a 20-bay frontage to the River Wensum was built, with a remarkable end turret accommodating the staircase. The venture failed, and the building passed into the hands of Jarrolds the printers who still occupy it. The great Carrow mustard works of J J Colman originated in 1854 and the complex contains many factory buildings in red and white brick of the late 19th century. The history of the company's principal product is displayed in Colman's Mustard Museum in Bridewell Alley. The Coslany iron bridge, constructed in 1804, is one of the oldest surviving iron bridges. Local industries are well represented in the Castle and Bridewell museums.

Colman's mustard was packaged in all shapes and sizes

NOTTINGHAM, *Nottinghamshire*

Nottingham's prosperity during the Industrial Revolution was based on lace, hosiery and the coal of the surrounding countryside. The Castle Museum contains collections of many local products, including Nottingham-ware pottery. The industrial museum in Wollaton Park, 3 miles west of the city centre, includes lace-making machinery, a replica of a horse gin of the kind used to raise coal from Nottinghamshire pits and a working 19th-century steam beam engine.

At Papplewick 8 miles to the north a few buildings and many water courses remain of a large cotton-spinning complex built by the Robinson family and the Papplewick water-pumping station, with two beam engines of 1871, is decorated with tiles and stained glass, making it one of the most ornate temples of public health in Britain. At Ruddington, 4 miles south of the city, the Framework Knitters' Museum is situated in a group of buildings constructed as four tenanted homes for knitters in 1829. Twenty-three knitting frames have been collected of which 12 still operate and are demonstrated from time to time.

SHARDLOW, *Derbyshire*

Shardlow was one of the principal canal ports of the Industrial Revolution, although unlike Stourport, Runcorn or Goole, it never grew into a

crane and canalside inns. The Clock Warehouse built in 1780 is now open as a restaurant.

The Clock Warehouse at one of Shardlow's canal basins

town. It is situated on the Trent and Mersey Canal, opened from Preston Brook near Runcorn in 1777, a mile west of the junction of the canal with the Trent at Derwentmouth. At this point the canal is crossed by the A6 road, which in the late 18th century formed the main route from London to Manchester. Goods brought up the Trent were transferred at Shardlow from broad river barges to canal narrow boats.

Shardlow was also one of the principal interchange points for the flyboat services operated by companies like Pickford and Henshalls which carried small consignments across the country, some of Shardlow's warehouses acting as 'sorting offices' for the various canal networks. When railways took most of this traffic in the mid-19th century most of the large warehouses at Shardlow were converted to corn mills, but it is still possible to identify warehouses used for malt, iron and salt, as well as a boatyard, cast-iron mileposts, a wharf

SHREWSBURY, *Shropshire*

Shrewsbury has always been a market town rather than a manufacturing centre, but just north of the station in Ditherington is one of the world's most important industrial buildings. It was designed by Charles Bage, and built as a flax mill in 1796—7. It was the first building to have a frame entirely of iron, with brick arches springing from iron crossbeams carrying the upper floors. It was converted to a maltings in 1886, when many of the windows were filled in. Malting ceased there in 1987. The Shrewsbury Canal from Trench was opened while the mill was under construction. When the canal was linked to the national system in 1835, a wholesale market for butter and cheese was built at its terminus in Howard Street. Its imposing frontage is in the classical style. Behind it is an extensive room for trading whilst underneath is a brick-vaulted 'crypt'. The building later became a railway warehouse and after a period of neglect is now a nightclub.

STOKE-ON-TRENT, *Staffordshire*
Stoke-on-Trent, the legendary 'five towns' of Arnold Bennett's novels, actually consists of six towns — Stoke, Hanley, Burslem, Fenton, Longton and Tunstall — which were amalgamated as the city of Stoke-on-Trent in 1908. It was in this area, in the coalfield in the broad valley of the River Trent, that the manufacture of pottery was transformed from a craft into a large-scale industry in the course of the 18th century. The Trent and Mersey Canal,

The Potteries in their prime

opened in 1777, runs like a spine through the area. A walk along the towpath provides some of the best impressions of the industrial landscape of the region.

The City Museum in Bethesda Street, Hanley, houses one of the world's great collections of ceramics, and should be one of the first priorities of any visit to the Potteries. The history of pottery manufacture in north Staffordshire from the 17th century to the present is illustrated with hundreds of magnificent pieces. Two other museum projects provide a close acquaintance with the conditions under which pottery was manufactured. The Gladstone Pottery Museum at Longton is located in a traditional 'potbank',

The Gladstone Pottery's bottle kiln

which has a formal frontage along the main road to Uttoxeter and a clutter of workshops and bottle ovens in the yard behind. The Etruscan Bone Mills, shortly to be opened as an out-station by the City Museum, date from the 1850s. Here a steam engine worked a series of grinding pans to produce the powdered bone necessary for the making of bone china.

The best-known figure in the history of the Potteries is Josiah Wedgwood, whose revolutionary works at Etruria were opened in 1769. A puzzling round building is all that remains at Etruria but demonstrations of pottery manufacture, a collection of wares and historical displays can be seen at the Wedgwood Centre at the modern factory in Barlaston. There are also visitor centres at the Coalport, Minton and Doulton works. The Chatterley Whitfield Mining Museum provides a vivid introduction to the coal industry on which the prosperity of pottery manufacture depended.

STOURBRIDGE, *West Midlands*
Stourbridge has long been Britain's
main centre for making decorative
glass. The industry still flourishes, and
it is possible to see glass being made,
to buy pieces from comprehensive
displays in factory shops and to study
something of the archaeology of the
industry. The best starting point is the
Red House Glassworks of Stuart
Crystal on the A491 at Wordsley, north
of Stourbridge. The outstanding
attraction here is an English glass cone
(see introduction), one of only four
which survive, part of a works built in
the late 18th century. The kiln is open
to the public as part of a series of
displays illustrating the history of the
Stourbridge glass industry. The Red
House works stand alongside a flight
of locks on the Dudley Canal, the
towpath of which offers some
impressive views of the region's
industrial landscape. The best displays

*The English glass cone of Red House Glassworks beside
the Dudley Canal*

of locally made glass are in the
Broadfield House Glass Museum at
Kingswinford. Local information offices
can provide up-to-date lists of factory
shops and details of where to see
glass-making demonstrations.

STOURPORT, *Hereford and Worcester*
Stourport was one of the new towns of
the Industrial Revolution. There was
no settlement of any consequence at
the point where the River Stour joins
the Severn until 1772 when the
Staffordshire and Worcestershire Canal
was opened. This canal linked the
Severn with the Trent and Mersey
Canal at Great Heywood near Stafford,
and, incidentally, with the whole of the
growing narrow canal network of the
Midlands. Basins were constructed at
the end of the canal where goods could

*By the late 1770s, Stourport had become a busy terminus
for canal and river traffic*

be transferred from the 4.2m-wide
barges used on the Severn to the
narrow boats employed on the canals
which were up to 2.1m in beam.

The first of the basins was
completed in 1771. Two sets of locks,
one for narrow boats and one wide
enough to accommodate river barges,
linked the basins with the Severn.
Warehouses, stables and an inn were
built around the basins, a bridge was
constructed and a town of elegant brick
Georgian houses grew up in the
vicinity. Stourport is the best preserved
of the canal ports of the Industrial
Revolution, a town still rich in
atmosphere although its basins are
now filled with pleasure craft rather
than barges and narrow boats.

THE NORTH COUNTRY

The phrase 'the industrial north' is something which glides easily from the tongue, and many people have an image of the north as an endless series of factory towns straddling the M62. Certainly no area was more thoroughly transformed by the Industrial Revolution than the valleys extending down from the Pennines into Lancashire and West Yorkshire. Areas which had previously supported only a relatively sparse population of domestic textile workers and farmers developed into towns and industrial villages, and the most remote valleys became populated.

One of the best ways to appreciate the impact of industry on the north is to drive along one of the old main roads across the Pennines like the A646 from Burnley to Sowerby Bridge, or the A58 from Rochdale

Liverpool became the north's most important port during the Industrial Revolution

to Halifax. Such roads provide rich selections of domestic textile buildings and mills of all periods from the small water-powered factories of the 18th century to the large steel-framed complexes of the 20th. Industry in the north, of course, means more than textiles. Coal has been one of the bases of the region's past prosperity. Metalworking and engineering have been of major importance, both in remote areas like the leadworkings in west Durham and the copper mines of the Lake District, and in cities like Sheffield and Newcastle.

NEWCASTLE UPON TYNE
CAUSEY BEAMISH
KILLHOPE
RYHOPE

CONISTON
STOTT PARK
DUDDON

FLEETWOOD
BINGLEY LEEDS
BRADFORD
CAPHOUSE
HELMSHORE
MANCHESTER

YORK

PORT SUNLIGHT LIVERPOOL
ELLESMERE PORT
SHEFFIELD
NORTHWICH STYAL MACCLESFIELD

0 10 20 30 mls
0 10 20 30 40 50 kms

BEAMISH, *Co Durham*

Beamish, approached off the A6076 north of Stanley, is an open-air museum — the European Museum of the Year in 1987 — which portrays in an exciting form the way of life of the people of the north-east during the period when the region was in the forefront of industrial development. There is a complete railway station complex, including stone-built 'cells' (typical of the north-east) where coal and lime were stored after being unloaded from hopper waggons. A North Eastern Railway class C 0—6—0 built at Gateshead in 1889 is among the working locomotives at the museum. There is a steam winding engine dating from 1855, of a type common in the north-east, which forms the centrepiece of a colliery complex. It is possible to go into a real drift mine, first dug in the 1850s, and to experience the living conditions of north-eastern miners in a row of pit cottages built in the 1860s. A working replica of George Stephenson's *Locomotion* of 1825 is steamed from time to time, and pulls trains of traditional chaldron (coal) waggons. Tramcars convey visitors around the museum, which also features a restored 1920s High Street with three shops, a pub, dentist's surgery, printer's workshop and solicitor's office.

BINGLEY, *West Yorkshire*

Bingley is a small industrial town some 5 miles north-west of Bradford on the A650. It is best known for the 'Five Rise', a flight of locks on the Leeds and Liverpool Canal designed by John Longbotham and built by the local stonemasons Barnabas Morvil, Jonathan Farrer, John Sugden and

Bingley's watery staircase of locks

William Wild in 1774. Signposts direct visitors to a car park from which the locks can be approached along the towpath past the smaller 'three-rise' staircase. The Leeds and Liverpool Canal, one of the most ambitious waterways projected during the Industrial Revolution, was authorised in 1770. It was not completed until 1816, but long before that time some parts were busy with local traffic, including the section through Bingley which was opened in 1774, an event commemorated by a plaque on the towpath. Most canal locks have pounds in between, but on the 'five rise', which lifts boats approximately 20m, the chambers of the locks open directly into each other. This method of construction saved on building costs, although it does cause delays because most craft cannot pass on the flight.

BRADFORD, *West Yorkshire*

Bradford was one of the most rapidly growing towns of the Industrial Revolution, its population increasing from only 13,000 in 1801 to 104,000 in 1851. It became the centre of the world's woollen trade, earning the nickname of 'Worstedopolis'. Much of the city centre has been redeveloped, but many outstanding buildings remain as reminders of the city's industrial heritage. 'Little Germany', to the east of the city centre, is a precinct of warehouses which developed from the 1850s, many of them being occupied by foreign and particularly by German merchants. The centre of Bradford's commercial life was the Wool Exchange, a Gothic building constructed between 1864 and 1867. The most impressive of the surviving mills in Bradford itself is the six-storey Manningham Mill built by Listers in 1873.

The best introduction to Bradford's industrial past is provided by the Industrial Museum in Moorside Road, Eccleshill, which is housed in Moorside Mills, a typical worsted spinning complex of 1875. Here you can learn about textile machinery by watching it in operation and talking to the demonstrators, and there are displays relating to the great variety of other products manufactured by the industries of Bradford.

About 4 miles north of Bradford just off the A650 is Saltaire, one of the most impressive industrial villages in England. It was begun in 1851 by Sir Titus Salt, who had already made a fortune as a textile manufacturer in Bradford itself. Its name is a combination of that of its founder and the River Aire which flows through the valley to the north. The great mill, as long as St Paul's Cathedral, was at the time of its construction amongst the largest in England. The houses were some of the most spacious ever built for working people at that time, and the streets take their names from Sir Titus's family and associates. Communal buildings include a school, an institute, a hospital and a Congregational church.

Saltaire, an industrial village on a grand scale

A 19th-century woollen mill beside the Leeds and Liverpool Canal at Leeds

A steam pump at the Bradford Industrial Museum

Cotton was shipped into and migrants poured out of Liverpool's historic waterfront during its heyday

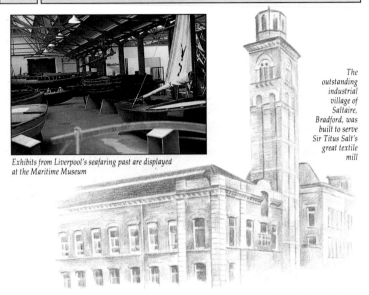

Exhibits from Liverpool's seafaring past are displayed at the Maritime Museum

The outstanding industrial village of Saltaire, Bradford, was built to serve Sir Titus Salt's great textile mill

Grassy, pleasant surroundings at Port Sunlight

The spectacular Venetian-style carpet mill of James Templeton and Company on Glasgow Green

Stained glass, People's Palace, Glasgow

A lock on the Caledonian Canal

Top left: *New Lanark, Robert Owen's ambitious 'model village'*
Top right: *Winding gear at the Lady Victoria Colliery, near Prestongrange*
Middle left: *Arbroath harbour*
Below: *The Forth's road and rail bridges (see South Queensferry, page 113)*

CAPHOUSE, *West Yorkshire*
Caphouse Colliery on the A642 at
Overton near Wakefield is being
developed as the Yorkshire Mining
Museum. The coalfield of the West
Riding has historically been amongst
the most important in Britain, and
Caphouse Colliery, with a history
of two centuries, was one of the
longest-lived of its mines. In its present
form it is a typical 19th-century mine,
although it has some 20th-century
additions, including pithead baths. Its
wooden headgear was one of the last
examples to remain in use in Britain. A
small stone-built engine house contains
a twin-cylinder horizontal steam
winding engine, built by Davy Bros in
1876, which operated until the early
1980s. Visitors are able to go 120m
underground, with safety helmet,
caplamp, self-rescuer and safety check
tokens, to see the workings under the
guidance of experienced miners.

Today and yesterday: compare the Causey Arch since its restoration with the bridge (below) as it was in the early 19th century

CAUSEY, *Co Durham*
About 2 miles north of Stanley off the
A6076 is the world's oldest surviving
railway bridge. Two distinct forms of
railway evolved in Britain in the course
of the 17th century, one in the
Shropshire coalfield around the
Ironbridge Gorge and the other in the
coalfield of Northumberland and
County Durham. The railways of the
latter system were generally of broader
gauge than those in the Midlands.

The bridge at Causey, known
locally as the Causey Arch, has a span
of 32m and is 24m high. It was built by
a local mason, Ralph Wood, in 1727, to
carry a railway across the Tanfield Beck
en route to the River Tyne. Its sheer
scale is evidence of the importance of
railways in the coalfield long before the
time of George Stephenson. The stone-
faced embankments approaching the
arch are almost as impressive as the
bridge itself. A footpath now crosses
the Causey Arch and others make it
easy to gain a good view of it from
below. A replica of a chaldron (coal)
waggon of the type which once used it
is exhibited at one end.

An engraving of Causey Arch, published in 1804

CONISTON, *Cumbria*

Coniston, in the heart of the Lake District, is the starting point for a walk through one of the most exciting industrial landscapes in Britain. The Copper Mines Valley is to the north-west of the village in the area drained by the Church Beck, and lies to the

The stylish, 19th-century passenger steam yacht Gondola *operates on Coniston Water*

south of Coniston Fells and north-east of the Old Man of Coniston. An excellent trail guide to the area can be obtained in shops in the village, where there is an extensive car park.

The copper mines of Coniston were worked from the 16th century until well into the 20th. The industry gained much of its power from the water flowing through the valley, which was used for pumping out mines as well as for dressing ore. Most of the surviving buildings date from a period of expansion between 1830 and 1855 and include a powder magazine, a sawmill, the mine manager's office (now the Youth Hostel), and a row of cottages supposedly built for Irish workmen. A steam boat operates from the pier in Coniston during the summer months.

DUDDON, *Cumbria*

The blast furnace at Duddon is amongst the best preserved in Britain. The furnace is situated in woodland to the west of the road which runs northwards from the A595 just west of Duddon Bridge between Broughton in Furness and Hallthwaites, a short distance from the A595. The furnace was built in 1736 to take advantage of local supplies of iron ore and of the abundant charcoal which could be obtained from the woodlands in the vicinity. The furnace itself is almost complete and it is possible to go right

The 18th-century Duddon Iron Furnace is now being conserved by the Lake District National Park

to the top of the structure. Behind the furnace are the ore store and a huge charcoal barn, while alongside are the remains of the water-power system which operated the furnace's bellows. In front can be seen the area where the molten iron was let out twice every day into the pig bed. Along the lane which leads past the furnace are several cottages in which the ironworkers were once housed.

ELLESMERE PORT, *Cheshire*

Ellesmere Port was one of the new 'canal towns' created during the Industrial Revolution. The Ellesmere Canal was launched in 1793 in the small north Shropshire town of Ellesmere, with the intention of linking the Mersey, the Dee and the Severn.

Early 19th-century warehouses, destroyed by fire in the 1970s. The Boat Museum now occupies adjacent basins and warehouses

The first portion to be built was that across the Wirral Peninsula from Chester to the Mersey, and the name Ellesmere Port was given to the settlement which grew up where the canal reached the river.

Its importance was successively increased in 1835 when the Shropshire Union Canal from Nantwich to Wolverhampton provided a direct link with the Midlands, and in 1894 when the Manchester Ship Canal was opened. The Boat Museum adjacent to junction 9 on the M53 provides an introduction to the port and to the history of inland waterways generally. The collection of about 60 vessels includes a 'starvationer', a boat of slim appearance which was used within the Duke of Bridgewater's mines at Worsley, some typical narrow boats of the Midlands canal system, and some wide barges used on the Leeds and Liverpool Canal.

FLEETWOOD, *Lancashire*

Fleetwood, at the mouth of the Rive Wyre, is a magnificent memorial to frustrated ambitions. Sir Peter Hesketh Fleetwood employed the celebrated architect Decimus Burton to lay out spacious streets and terraces around the terminus of a branch railway from Preston opened in 1840. It was anticipated that travellers from London to Scotland might go by rail to Fleetwood and then by sea to Glasgow. Burton built the North Euston Hotel to cater for their needs, and two lighthouses were constructed to guide packet ships into the estuary.

Queen Victoria used this route when returning from Scotland to London in 1847, but the opening of the railway over Shap Fell brought an end to this traffic. Fleetwood's prosperity revived from the 1870s with its growth as a fishing port. The Museum of the

Fleetwood was more successful as a fishing port than ferry terminus

Fishing Industry in Dock Street provides an introduction to the town's history, and two particularly commendable transport experiences are the tram ride across the cliffs to Blackpool and the ferry over the mouth of the Wyre to Knott End-on-Sea.

HELMSHORE, *Lancashire*

The Museum of the Lancashire Textile Industry at Helmshore, on the B6235 about a mile south-west of Haslingden and 7 miles north of Bury, provides a superb introduction to an industry of crucial historical importance. The museum is housed in a mill which in its present form dates from 1859—60, an earlier structure having been destroyed by fire.

Spinning cotton within the Museum of the Lancashire Textile Industry

On the ground floor visitors can see the complete range of machines including a six-cylinder breaking-up machine (often called a devil), and a single-cylinder pickering machine and scutcher which cleaned and disentangled the cotton. On the first floor is a set of breaker carding engines which combed the cotton in preparation for spinning, and a magnificent range of cotton mules, each of which spins 714 strands of yarn. Seeing the mules in operation alone justifies a long journey to Helmshore. In the adjacent Higher Mill, fulling, milling and other processes for finishing cloth can be observed. A collection of early textile machinery includes a spinning jenny and a water frame from Arkwright's mill at Cromford.

KILLHOPE, *Co Durham*

The western parts of County Durham, particularly the valleys of the Wear, the Nent and the East and West Alen, are rich in the remains of lead mining and smelting. Smelter chimneys, dressing floors and terraces of workers' cottages can be found throughout the region. The most spectacular monument of the lead industry in this area is the ore-crushing mill at Killhope on the A689, about 2 miles north-west of Cowshill and about 6 miles east of Alston.

The site is dominated by a vast iron waterwheel, 10.2m in diameter and 2m wide, which was installed in 1876—8 to drive four sets of crushing rollers. The crushing plant itself has

Water power was harnessed by this huge wheel at Killhope's lead ore crushing plant

been scrapped although the buildings which housed it still stand. The ore was obtained from local mines, of which the entrance to one, the Park Level, can be seen nearby. It appears that the ore found in the vicinity was too hard to be broken by hand, which accounts for the construction of this water-powered plant by the Beaumont Company in the 1860s. The whole site with its water-power system, crushing plant and mine shop is being restored to its working condition of the 1870s.

LEEDS, *West Yorkshire*

Leeds, on the borders of the Yorkshire coalfield and the Pennine textile region, and at the head of navigation on the River Aire, developed during the 18th century into the commercial centre of the Yorkshire textile industry. Many of the city's industrial workers lived in back-to-back houses, which were still being built into the 20th century.

These terraces, built around 1890 at Armley, are typical examples of working people's housing built in Leeds during the 19th century

The Leeds Industrial Museum is at Armley Mills, just south of the A65, a little more than a mile from the city centre. There was a fulling mill at Armley from the second half of the 17th century, but the mill in its present form dates largely from a rebuilding by Benjamin Gott, one of the most eminent of Leeds's textile masters, in the first decade of the 19th century.

There are extensive displays of textile machinery, as well as a collection of early steam engines, and exhibits relating to the clothing industry. The museum publishes a trail guide to sites of interest along the canal towpaths between Armley and the city centre, and northwards towards Kirkstall Abbey.

Leeds was the principal centre of the flax industry in England, new methods of manufacture having been pioneered by John Marshall from the 1790s. In 1838—40 Marshall's company built a remarkable mill in the Egyptian style, designed by Ignatius Bonomi. It still stands in Marshall Street and has been used by a mail order firm. Nearby is T W Harding's pin works which includes a chimney of 1864 modelled on the tower of the Palazzo de Signore in Verona, and a square dust-extraction tower which is a copy of Giotto's campanile at the Duomo in Florence.

Leeds was one of the leading centres in Britain for the manufacture of architectural ceramics, the principal area of production being at Burmantofts east of the centre. The Metropole Hotel and Kirkgate Market display some of the dazzling products of this industry.

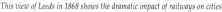

This view of Leeds in 1868 shows the dramatic impact of railways on cities

LIVERPOOL, *Merseyside*

Liverpool was the premier port of northern England during the Industrial Revolution. It gained its prosperity through the sugar, cotton, tobacco and slave trades in the 18th century, and became the chief port in Europe for the despatch of migrants to America in the 19th. The first dock was completed as early as 1734, but the main period of dock construction took place between 1824 and 1860 under the direction of Jesse Hartley. By 1900 docks extended 4 miles north and 3 miles south of Pierhead, and the city's pre-eminence at that time is shown by the splendour of the main buildings located on the waterfront — the Royal Liver Building, the Cunard Building and the offices of the port authority — all put up between 1900 and 1914.

return to economic vitality of the Merseyside region after the ravages of the depression of the early 1980s. Part of the complex is occupied by the Merseyside Maritime Museum which has extensive displays on the workings of the port, while the rest is occupied by shops, offices and a branch of the Tate Gallery. The pump house which provided hydraulic power to the dock has been converted to a pub.

The world's first main-line railway was the Liverpool and Manchester Railway opened in 1830. Some traces can still be seen near Edgehill Station, and at Rainhill, 9 miles to the east (scene, incidentally, of the famous locomotive trials of

Liverpool's waterfront architecture expresses turn-of-the-century pride and prosperity in stone

The centrepiece of Liverpool's dockland is the Albert Dock complex, built by Hartley between 1841 and 1845. The five-storey warehouse buildings are iron-framed, with the walls carried on elliptical arches springing from cast-iron columns. This complex is now the symbol of the slow

1829), is the remarkable skew bridge shown in early views of the line. Liverpool Museum in William Brown Street includes the locomotive *Lion*, built for the Liverpool and Manchester Railway in 1838 (though the loco is sometimes away on touring exhibitions).

MACCLESFIELD, *Cheshire*

Macclesfield was one of the chief centres of the silk industry in Britain during the Industrial Revolution. The town's landscape is still dominated by large mills in the classical style and by terraces of weavers' cottages, with loom shops on the top floors. The best starting point for a visit to Macclesfield is the heritage centre in the Sunday School, a vast building erected in 1813, when Sunday Schools were important in the education of adults.

Restored weavers' cottages — note the attic workshop windows — in Paradise Street

The most impressive mills are Frosts Mill on Park Green, which dates from the late 18th century, and was originally water-powered, and the Card Factory on the Chester Road, built as a steam-powered mill in the 1820s. The best-known silk weavers' cottages are those which have been restored in Paradise Street, but many other examples can be found in the town, some of them three-storey buildings towering out of two-storey terraces. There are regular demonstrations of silk weaving at Paradise Mill in Park Lane.

MANCHESTER, *Greater Manchester*

Manchester was the classic city of the Industrial Revolution, the place which in the 1840s came to epitomise all that was wrong with the factory system and the urban growth it created. Charles Dickens, Friedrich Engels, Mrs Gaskell and many other writers, British and foreign, visited the city and wrote about their impressions of it.

During the 18th century Manchester became the chief commercial centre of the Lancashire cotton trade, and with the introduction of steam power into factories it developed as a considerable manufacturing centre in its own right. In the course of the 19th century its engineering industry grew rapidly, and companies in the city supplied locomotives and textile machinery to customers throughout the world. Manchester was also the focus of the canal system of the north-west, and the towpaths of the canals which criss-cross the centre are one of the best means of gaining an acquaintance with the city's industrial past.

Manchester's iron viaduct, the architecture of the Railway Age on a grandiose scale

Cavernous cotton factories once lined Manchester's Union Street

Manchester's role as a commercial centre is best understood by a visit to the Exchange, now a theatre, or to Whitworth Street, which is given a cavernous appearance by lines of tall warehouses where merchants once inspected the varieties of fabric manufactured in Lancashire. The former Central Station, built in 1876—9 with a single-arch train shed 64m in span and a spectacular brick-vaulted undercroft, has been splendidly restored after years of disuse, and is now the G-Mex Exhibition Centre. The Great North Railway warehouses alongside were a remarkable transfer point between rail, road and water transport, while the terracotta Midland Hotel of 1898 is one of Britain's most spectacular railway hotels.

Castlefield, at the terminus of the Duke of Bridgewater's Canal which was opened in 1765, is the best starting point for the study of Manchester's industrial past. The area is dominated by warehouses and by railway viaducts and bridges, the latter notable for their decorative ironwork. The Greater Manchester Museum of Science and Industry incorporates Liverpool Road Station, the original terminus of the Liverpool and Manchester Railway (opened in 1830) and the world's oldest railway passenger station. The iron and glass Lower Campsfield Market Hall of 1876—7 now houses an aerospace display. The 'power hall' includes locomotives and stationary steam engines, many of them the products of Manchester companies. The textiles section includes an Arkwright carding engine of 1800. Visitors are able to see work in progress in the museum's conservation department.

Castlefield is linked by the Rochdale Canal (opened in 1805) to Ancoats, where there are many early 19th-century warehouses grouped around the canal basins in Ducie Street and Dale Street. Beyond them stand several important canalside mills, including Sedgewick Mill, designed by William Fairbairn for McConnell and

The yacht Norseman *celebrates the opening of the Manchester Ship Canal in 1894*

Kennedy and completed in 1820. The engineer William Fairbairn was one of the great figures of Victorian Manchester. He arrived in the city in 1814 and went into business manufacturing iron waterwheels, steam boilers and constructional ironwork. He was the author of several books on the use of iron in engineering, and a consultant on major projects throughout the country. In Oldham Road is Victoria Square, a five-storey, red-brick apartment block erected as a slum clearance project in 1889.

The Manchester Ship Canal, opened in 1894, made Manchester a port for ocean-going ships, but it has declined since the 1970s though there are plans for dockland redevelopment.

NEWCASTLE UPON TYNE,
Tyne and Wear

Newcastle upon Tyne is the metropolis of north-east England, and the centre of Britain's historically most important coalfield. The city stands at the lowest bridging point on the Tyne, and in the 19th century, together with Gateshead on the southern bank of the river, it prospered as a port for the shipping of coal. It was also one of the world's principal engineering centres, specialising in shipbuilding, railway rolling stock and armaments.

The Tyne bridges form one of the most breathtaking of all industrial landscapes. They can easily be surveyed from several points along the river banks, but one of the most exciting views is that seen from a train on the newest of the bridges carrying the Tyneside Metro. The oldest of the surviving bridges is Robert Stephenson's double-deck High Level Bridge of 1845—9 which carries the

Three ways to cross the Tyne: the double-deck High Level Bridge and, below it, the Swing Bridge

main-line railway on six cast-iron arches with a roadway suspended beneath. The Swing Bridge was built in 1876 by Lord Armstrong. It retains its original hydraulic pumps but they are now electrically operated.

The Museum of Science and Engineering is in Blandford Square. It includes displays on most aspects of Tyneside's industrial history and features the work of its pioneers, amongst whom are George Stephenson, Charles Parsons and Lord Armstrong.

Dunston Staithes, 2 miles west of the centre on the south bank of the river, is a site typical of the installations used in the north-east to transfer coal from railway waggons to the holds of ships. Built in 1890 by the North Eastern Railway, and some 500m long, the staithes are now preserved as an industrial monument. About 3 miles further west at Lemington is one of Britain's few surviving glass cones.

A miner at work in a 13-inch seam at the Lilly Drift Mine, near Newcastle

NORTHWICH, *Cheshire*

Salt is the most important of the native raw materials used by the British chemical industry. Cheshire has for centuries been the chief source of salt in Britain, and during the course of the 19th century Northwich became the principal centre of production in the country. It is now largely dominated by the huge plants of ICI which provide a vast range of materials for industry. The Salt Museum on London Road is located in a former workhouse, and houses extensive displays of salt-working equipment.

Filling tubs of salt in the old works

A mile north-west of Northwich, the River Weaver is linked with the Trent and Mersey Canal by the Anderton Lift, one of the outstanding canal monuments in Britain. It was constructed to the design of Edward Leader Williams in 1872—5, and converted from hydraulic to electrical operation in 1903—8.

PORT SUNLIGHT, *Merseyside*

Port Sunlight is the most spectacular of the garden suburbs created by late Victorian industrialists around their factories. W H Lever, the successful manufacturer of Sunlight Soap, had a works at Warrington but in 1888 moved to a new site on a creek off the Mersey about 3 miles south of Birkenhead. Around his new factory some of the best known architects in Britain were employed to design houses in a bewildering variety of styles, some modelled on the traditional timber buildings of Cheshire, some on Continental precedents. Lever also built assembly

Mock-Tudor at Port Sunlight

rooms, institutes and other meeting halls, together with a school and a Congregational church. The Bridge Inn, modelled on an Elizabethan original, was originally a temperance hotel. The best starting point for a visit to Port Sunlight is the heritage centre near the railway station. On the eastern side of the A41 is Bromborough Pool Village, a small model settlement of an earlier era, built when Price's Candle Company moved from Battersea to Merseyside in the 1850s.

RYHOPE, *Co Durham*

Ryhope Pumping Station is situated just west of the A1018 some 3 miles south of Sunderland. The station is one of Britain's most remarkable 'palaces of public health', a place where it is possible to gain some idea of just how much it meant to the Victorians to have clean and healthy supplies of drinking water. It was built by the Sunderland and South Shields Water Company, which was formed in 1852.

The pumping station, built in imposing — almost intimidating — style

The company built a succession of pumping stations along the outcrop of magnesian limestone in the eastern part of County Durham. Work on the station at Ryhope commenced in 1865, and it came into use in 1868. Two double-acting, compound, rotative beam engines were supplied by Messrs R W Hawthorn of Newcastle, and they were originally provided with steam by six Cornish boilers. The engines worked until 1967, and the station is now in the hands of a trust which opens it to the public. The buildings are set in a garden amid lawns, flower beds and trees, and surrounded by three reservoirs, one of which was covered in 1956 to prevent contamination by falling leaves.

SHEFFIELD, *South Yorkshire*
Sheffield, at the confluence of the rivers Sheaf and Don, is one of the world's principal centres for the manufacture of cutlery and edge tools. The city rose to prosperity in the 18th century through an abundance of water power and coal, access to navigable water and the ease with which high-quality iron from the Baltic countries and Scandinavia could be imported. In the late 19th century a series of large steel works specialising in armaments grew up on the banks of the Don.

Sheffield's industrial history is well illustrated in its museums. The Industrial Museum on Kelham Island is located in the former power station for the city's tramway system, and provides a comprehensive picture of working life in the city over the past 300 years. There is a courtyard of workshops of the type occupied by the 'little mesters', the outworkers who carried on many of the processes in the cutlery industry. The vast 12,000 hp

River Don engine, formerly used in an armour plate mill, regularly turns.

The industrial hamlet at Abbeydale on the A621 to the south of the city is a group of late 18th-century cottages and workshops on the Sheaf, which includes grinding shops for scythes, water-powered tilt hammers, and a crucible steel shop where the process invented by Benjamin Huntsman in 1740 can be observed. Wortley Top Forge off the A629 9 miles north of the city is an old ironworks with a breast-shot waterwheel, a helve hammer and three jib cranes. Remains of cementation furnaces for making steel can be seen near Sheffield's centre in Hoyle Street and Russell Street, while at Catcliffe 4 miles to the east, just off the M1, is an English glass cone built about 1740.

At Elsecar on the B6097 some 7 miles north is the only Newcomen engine in Britain which still stands in the house for which it was built. It was constructed in about 1795 by John Burgh of Chesterfield.

HELVE HAMMER

The waterwheel provided the power to drive the hammer repeatedly down on to the anvil

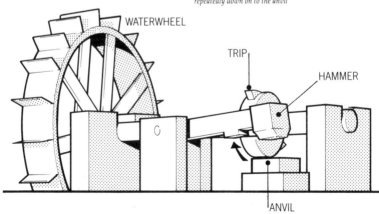

WATERWHEEL

TRIP

HAMMER

ANVIL

STOTT PARK, *Cumbria*

Stott Park Bobbin Mill, on the western side of Lake Windermere, about 2 miles north of the A590 at Newby Bridge, is perhaps the best place in Britain at which to gain an understanding of the importance of woodland industries during the Industrial Revolution. Stott Park and the many similar mills in the Lake District produced the bobbins and reels used in all branches of the textile industry in the north of England, as well as the humble 'cotton reel' used in the home. The mill still contains much of its 19th-century equipment, including lathes, polishing drums, saws and drying racks. Several of the machines were made by Lake District foundries like Fell of Windermere which specialised in such equipment. Power was provided by a small horizontal steam engine. The mill is surrounded by barns used for storing the coppice wood which was used for bobbins. The machinery is enthusiastically demonstrated by former bobbin makers.

Quarry Bank, a splendid Georgian mill complex restored as a working museum of the cotton industry

STYAL, *Greater Manchester*

Quarry Bank Mill, Styal, west of the B5166 about a mile north of Wilmslow, is the centre of the best-preserved textile factory colony in England. The mill complex was established in 1784 by an Ulsterman, Samuel Greg. By the 1840s it was one of the showpieces of the factory system, a place where critics of that system were urged to go to see how clean and healthy employment in textile manufacuring could be. Within the mill are displays incorporating many working machines which show the various processes used in the cotton textile industry.

The clean conditions which prevailed at Styal were due to the use of water power, and an impressively large waterwheel from a mill in Yorkshire is being restored and installed here. In the adjacent park it is possible to see a variety of houses built for the cotton workers, or converted for their use from older buildings. The National Trust has restored the Apprentice House, which once accommodated more than 100 child workers, and Styal Shop, originally opened by Samuel Greg and later operated by a Co-operative Society.

YORK, *North Yorkshire*

York is one of the great regional capitals of England, a walled city of ancient origins, crowned by a magnificent cathedral and containing architectural treasures of every period.

York's chief importance in the history of industrial Britain is as a railway centre, so it is a fitting location for the National Railway Museum.

Weatherill on the Stanhope and Tyne Railway, and Swannington on the Leicester and Swannington. There are several 19th-century royal coaches, and, by contrast, an open third-class carriage from the Bodmin and Wadebridge Railway. There are locomotives in profusion, three of the

The immaculate Green Arrow *was overhauled by the National Railway Museum*

York Station, which is still busy with trains and passengers, is itself an important industrial monument, with four magnificent curving arched roofs of iron and glass built by Thomas Prosser, Benjamin Burleigh and William Peachey in 1871—7. The National Railway Museum in Leman Road is located in the roundhouses of the former York locomotive depot. It possesses the richest collection of railway rolling stock and other equipment in the world, with many items which go back to the very dawn of the main-line railway system.

In the yard is the Gaunless Bridge of 1829 from the Stockton and Darlington Railway, perhaps the first of all iron railway bridges. From the days before locomotives were used on every section of railway there are stationary winding engines from

Locomotives in the museum's vast Main Hall

most interesting being the 0—4—0 *Agenoria* built for the Pensnett Railway in 1829, the London and North Western Railway's 2—2—2 *Columbine* of 1845, and the North Eastern Railway's 4—4—0 No 1621, built in 1892, which took part in the 'Races to the North' in 1895.

SCOTLAND

*T*he Central Lowlands of Scotland
underwent an Industrial Revolution in
the 18th century which was similar to that
in England. It grew in part from success in
international commerce, particularly that
of the port of Glasgow. The cotton textile
industry expanded rapidly in the west,
where two of its outstanding monuments
are the modest weaver's cottage at
Kilbarchan near Paisley, and the great
range of mills and tenements located
at New Lanark.

The south shore of the Firth of Forth
is a region of particular importance in
Scottish industrial history. Several of the
leading inventors and entrepreneurs of the
late 18th century worked there. It was the
location of Scotland's first modern

ironworks, the Carron Foundry. The region
is bisected by the Union Canal, with its
splendid aqueducts; this south shore also
has a landscape feature unique in Britain
— the great 'bings', waste tips of shale
which resulted from oil extraction in the
19th century. Much of the region is
dominated by the vast bulk of the Forth
Railway Bridge. One of the two British
gasworks to be preserved is at Biggar, while
Alloa possesses one of only four surviving
glass cones (see introduction, page 12).
Dundee, Edinburgh and Glasgow are rich
in industrial monuments, with patterns of
building quite distinct from those seen
in England.

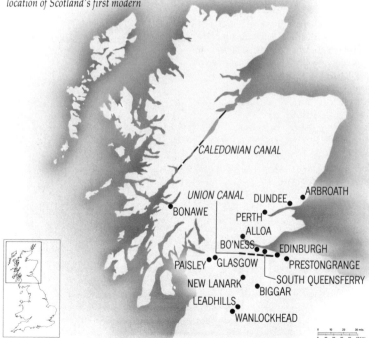

ALLOA, *Central*

Alloa is one of the busiest of Scotland's smaller industrial towns, with textile mills, breweries and a glassworks all active on the fringe of the centre. Alloa rose to importance in the 18th century as a coal port on the Forth, developed by the Earls of Mar whose mansion stood near the 15th-century Alloa Tower. Broad Street and Lime Tree Walk are the remnants of a formal route from Alloa to the harbour along the edge of the earl's baroque gardens. Two surviving gate piers are known to date from 1714.

Coal travelled to the harbour along a primitive railway, and it is still possible to walk along this 'wagon road' of 1768, from the end of Primrose Street alongside the Station Inn, through two brick-vaulted tunnels under the town centre, to emerge south of Bedford Place. The plant of United Glass Containers in Glasshouse Loan has developed from a glasshouse established in 1750 by Lady Frances Erskine. Amid the modern installations

Scotland's only surviving English glass cone

stands a 20m-high English glass cone built in 1825, the only one left in Scotland. The outstanding textile mill in the district is the six-storey, 25-bay Strude Mill of about 1820 at Alva.

ARBROATH, *Tayside*

Arbroath is a fishing port and textile town, largely built in red sandstone, and bisected by the East Coast Main Line. The present harbour was begun in 1725, and by 1740 vessels from Arbroath were trading with North America and the Baltic. It was extended from 1839, with further alterations in the 1870s, although most of its traffic was eventually lost to the railways, and in the present century it has been largely a fishing port.

The tall signal tower looking out across Arbroath harbour is now a museum

Arbroath 'Smokies' are world famous, and Seagate, north of the harbour, is a street of gaily painted single-storey buildings in which fish are gutted, dried and smoked. The harbour is full of interest and is one of the principal points on Scotland's Fishing Heritage Trail which has been developed by the Scottish Tourist Board. In the shipyards on either side of the harbour it is possible to see traditional methods of building and repairing wooden ships in use. Most of the former flax and sailcloth mills are in the area north of the station. Arbroath's museum, which provides an introduction to the town's industries, is situated in the signal tower, built in 1813 for the Bell Rock Lighthouse.

BIGGAR, *Strathclyde*

Biggar is a market town mostly built along a single wide main street. The town gasworks, begun in 1839 by the Biggar Gas Light Company, was typical of those found in every small town in Britain, but it was one of the last in Scotland to be closed when natural gas from the North Sea replaced coal gas. After it ceased operation in 1973 the works passed into the guardianship of the Scottish Development Department and the site is now a museum administered from the National Museums of Scotland located in Edinburgh.

In common with all other such establishments, the Biggar Gasworks burned coal in retorts, producing coal gas which was stored in gas holders, and coke which was sold as a by-product. The horizontal retorts survive

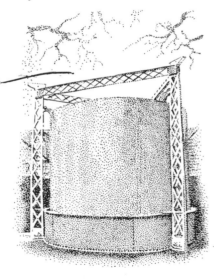

A gas holder which forms part of the preserved gasworks at Biggar

in a retort house dating from 1914, while the older retort house was latterly used as a coal store. There are two small gasholders dating from 1858 and 1880. A video provides an introduction to the history of the gas supply industry, and there is an exhibition of domestic gas appliances. The works are situated north of the A72 at the south-west end of the town on the east bank of the Biggar Brook, near the Cross Keys Hotel.

BONAWE, *Strathclyde*

Until the second half of the 18th century charcoal was the fuel most commonly used for the smelting of iron ore. It was a friable material, likely to be reduced to useless dust if it was transported over long distances. It was to utilise the charcoal which could be made in the forests of Argyll that Richard Ford and Co, who operated the Newland Ironworks near Ulverston in the Lake District, built a furnace in 1752—3 at Bonawe on the northern outskirts of Taynuilt which is on the A85, north of Oban. They made pig iron from ores imported from Furness and from central Scotland. The works operated until 1876, although only intermittently in the final decades.

The furnace complex at Bonawe is one of the best preserved in Europe. The furnace stack is complete, and the date 1753 is cast on the lintel of the tapping arch. The charcoal barn and ore shed, both built in the traditional style of the Lake District, still stand, and the waterwheel pit is intact, although the wheel itself has been removed. The slag heap area now forms the car park, and the manager's house and workers' cottages can be seen nearby.

BO'NESS, *Central*

Bo'Ness on the south bank of the Forth, was Scotland's third port in the 18th century. Many of the leading figures in the Industrial Revolution, among them James Watt, Lord Dundonald and John Roebuck, lived and worked in the vicinity. A series of industrial museums is being developed linked by the Bo'Ness and Kinneil Railway. The station at the east end of

Bo'Ness Station (above) and a Caledonian Railway 0—4—4T of 1907 steaming out of the station's reconstructed train shed

the town incorporates wrought-iron trusses and cast-iron columns from Haymarket in Edinburgh, the oldest train shed in Scotland. A clay mine at Birkhill is to be preserved, and the railway runs past the impressive headstocks of Kinneil Colliery. The wet dock of the port of Bo'Ness, now disused, is alongside the station, while the port's tobacco warehouse, built in 1772, is now the town library.

Kinneil House, home of the Dukes of Hamilton in the 17th century, and of Dr John Roebuck in the 18th, is open to the public, and in the stables there is a museum with displays of local industry, particularly potteries. In 1765, James Watt carried out some of his experiments on the steam engine in one of the outhouses.

CALEDONIAN CANAL, *Highland*

The Caledonian Canal was built under the direction of Thomas Telford between 1804 and 1822. Taking advantage of the lochs in the Great Glen, a route was created which enabled vessels of modest size needing to pass between the east and west coasts of Scotland to avoid the long and dangerous passage around the Pentland Firth. The towpaths are maintained in excellent condition and much of the route can be followed along the A82. The eastern end of the canal is near Clachnaharry on the Beauly Firth west of Inverness, where the workshops and single-storey houses for employees were built.

There are four locks at Muirtown, which was intended as a second harbour for Inverness. The route passes through Loch Ness to Fort Augustus where there are four locks, and then through Loch Oich and Loch Lochy. South of Gairlochy the canal crosses the River Loy on a granite aqueduct and at Moy there is the only remaining survivor of the original cast-iron swing bridges built along the canal. After passing down the spectacular flight of eight locks known as Neptune's Staircase to the north of Fort William the canal ends at Corpach at the head of Loch Linnhe.

DUNDEE, *Tayside*

The Tay Bridge from the Dundee side of the river

Dundee, at the mouth of the River Tay, was the capital of the British jute industry. In the mid-19th century many huge mills were constructed to spin and weave jute imported from India, which was used for sacking, carpets, linoleum and many other purposes. The industry has declined in recent decades but many impressive mill buildings remain. An industrial collection has been established in Dundee's Central Museum with the object of showing how jute was processed and how important it was in industry at large and in everyday life.

Most textile workers in Dundee lived in tenements of a distinctive type, many of which remain in use. Good examples can be seen in Hawkhill and in Bellefield Avenue, the latter dating from 1899.

Dundee is also an important port and its significance in maritime history is shown by the presence in the city of two historic vessels — the frigate *Unicorn*, built at Chatham in 1824, and the *Discovery* in which Captain Scott sailed for the South Pole in 1912.

Dundee is linked with Fife by the Tay Bridges. The present railway bridge was built to the designs of William Barlow between 1882 and 1887, replacing the bridge designed by Thomas Bouch, which was destroyed in a storm in 1879. Seventy-five lives were lost when a train fell through the gap where the girders had collapsed. The bridge, which carries the main line from Edinburgh to Aberdeen, is about 1½ miles long. There are excellent parking facilities on the riverside drive which forms the A85 along the north shore of the Firth, providing a magnificent view of the bridge. A terraced garden which is located in Perth Road just opposite the end of Airlie Place provides a higher and more spectacular viewpoint.

At Wormit on the Fife side of the bridge, the piers of the old bridge can be seen from the platform of the former station, just off the B946.

EDINBURGH, *Lothian*

The city's impressive North Bridge

A city of exceptional architectural riches, Edinburgh is celebrated for its elegant squares and its academic institutions rather than for its factories. Its industrial monuments are nevertheless of remarkable interest. Dean Village was Edinburgh's ancient milling area, and until 1970 was the site of the city's principal tannery. West Mill, dating from the early 19th century, is converted to housing, while the granary of Bell's Mills, destroyed by an explosion in 1975, is part of the Dragonara Hotel. Towering above the village is Telford's Dean Bridge of 1829, with four segmental arches each of 29m span carrying the roadway some 32m above the river bed.

In the pleasant old village of Cramond north-west of the centre, where the River Almond joins the Firth of Forth, there are several 18th-century ironworks. Some of the ironworkers' houses survive. Guided tours of the area begin in the Old Maltings.

Waverley Station, one of the most spectacular in Britain, was created between 1868 and 1874, replacing three previous stations and providing 12 through tracks. The overall glass roof is carried on lattice girders which rest on slim cast-iron columns. The station is crossed by Waverley Bridge and the North Bridge, massive structures of the mid-1890s, the latter carrying the magnificent North British Hotel, completed in 1902.

Edinburgh's first deepwater harbour consisted of the East and West Docks built by John Rennie in the first two decades of the 19th century. Only the entrance gate to the former survives, together with an orginal cast-iron swing bridge. A succession of other docks was constructed, from the Victoria Dock of 1847—51 to the Imperial Dock of 1896—8. The Italianate pumping station which operated hydraulic equipment in the docks stands to the north of the Prince of Wales Graving Dock.

The Royal Museum of Scotland (Chambers Street) houses the *Wylam Dilly* locomotive of 1813 and a Boulton and Watt steam engine of 1786. The Great Hall of the museum, built by Francis Fowke in 1861, is a remarkable composition in iron and glass some 82m long and 21m high.

GLASGOW, *Strathclyde*

Glasgow was the second city of the British Empire, a vast concentration of industry and people whose fortunes have mirrored closely the basic changes in the way Britain has earned its living over the past two-and-a-half centuries. In the 18th century Glasgow prospered as a port particularly well situated for trading with America. In the first part of the century the region specialised in the manufacture of fine linens. This made it a suitable area for the introduction of cotton weaving, which first supplemented and then supplanted linen production.

The first steam-powered cotton mill in the city was built in 1792, and textiles subsequently became one of Glasgow's most important manufactures. The outstanding surviving mill is a carpet manufactory, that of James Templeton and Son at 62 Templeton Street, overlooking Glasgow Green. The factory was established in 1857, incorporating parts of a cotton mill of the 1820s, but from 1888 a new block modelled on the Doge's Palace in Venice was built to the design of W Leiper. The mill was completed in 1892, and its bright polychrome brickwork and elaborate ornamentation make it one of the most colourful industrial buildings in the whole of Britain.

The growth of iron-making in Ayrshire and Lanarkshire to the south of Glasgow during the first half of the 19th century stimulated the growth of shipbuilding on the Clyde. In the 20th century this has remained the city's most celebrated industry, although it has contracted massively in recent decades. The best way in which to get some sense of its scale, and its past importance to Glasgow, is to explore the landscapes of cranes, fabrication shops and docks to be found on both banks of the Clyde downstream from the city centre.

Glaswegians used the Clyde for business and pleasure, travelling along the river to work and on recreational outings. Here, crowds are embarking at the bustling Broomielaw quayside, circa 1900

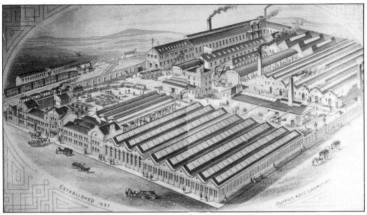

Neilson and Company's Hyde Park Works, established in 1837, boasted an 'output 4,000 locomotives'

Glasgow also became one of the principal centres in the world for the manufacture of locomotives during the second half of the 19th century. The North British and Caledonian Railways had their own works in the city, and several private locomotive builders amalgamated in 1903 to form the North British Locomotive Company Ltd, then the largest builders of railway locomotives in Europe. Most railway engineering concerns in Glasgow have long since closed, although it is possible to study some of their products at the Museum of Transport. The museum's collections include horse-drawn vehicles, tramcars, ship models and fire engines as well as a superb collection of typically Scottish locomotives.

Glasgow was the centre of the Scottish railway system, with four terminal stations, two of which, Buchanan Street and St Enoch, have disappeared during rationalisation. Glasgow's municipal underground railway, opened by a private company in 1896 and taken over by the corporation in 1923, remains in operation. Its St Enoch Station, a tasteful building in the Jacobean style in red sandstone designed by J Miller, is one of the most attractive railway buildings in Britain. It now serves as an information centre.

Working people in Glasgow traditionally lived in multi-storeyed tenement blocks, constructed from the local red sandstone. Such tenements can still be seen in the city, although many have been demolished. The Tenement House at 145 Buccleuch Street is a first-floor flat in a tenement block built in the 19th century, where the furnishings and possessions of a family who lived there more than 50 years ago are displayed to visitors. The social history of Glasgow again features at the People's Palace on Glasgow Green where there are collections relating to the political and social movements which flourished in the city in the late 19th and early 20th centuries. The museum also has displays of pottery, textiles, glass and metal castings.

LEADHILLS AND WANLOCKHEAD, *Strathclyde/ Dumfries and Galloway*

The remote and frequently rain-swept villages of Wanlockhead and Leadhills in the Lowther Hills were once known as 'God's treasure house in Scotland'. The most dramatic approach is by the B7040 from Elvanfoot, along the valley of the Elvan Water, past a disused bridge and a remarkable curving viaduct of the branch railway which once served the villages. For a radius of several miles around Wanlockhead the landscape is dominated by the waste tips and dressing floors of lead, silver and gold mines. In the centre of Wanlockhead is the Museum of Scottish Lead Mining, from which tours of a nearby mine are organised in the summer season. Less than $\frac{1}{2}$ mile away along the road which runs towards Meadowfoot Cemetery is a water balance pump used for draining the mines. It has the appearance of a steam-worked beam engine, and is probably the only such engine in Britain remaining *in situ*.

The rare water balance pump

Both villages abound in brightly painted terraces of single-storey cottages, once occupied by miners. In Leadhills is the Miners' Reading Society Library, founded in 1756.

NEW LANARK, *Strathclyde*

New Lanark, by the Falls of Clyde, is one of the world's most evocative industrial monuments. Richard Arkwright and David Dale established cotton mills powered by water from the Falls of Clyde in the narrow wooded gorge cut by the river south of the old town of Lanark in 1785. By 1800, 2,500 people were living in the

A view over New Lanark's tenement roofs to Robert Owen's school, completed in 1817

adjacent village. In that year Robert Owen, a native of Newtown in Wales, arrived at New Lanark and subsequently became a partner with David Dale. He applied there his ideas for the development of harmony within industrial society. The nursery founded in the Nursery Buildings (constructed in 1809), the adult education provided in the Institution for the Formation of Character (built in 1816), the imaginative teaching methods in the school (built in 1817), and the co-operative principles applied in the village store, were all noble concepts many years ahead of their time. Since 1974, an ambitious programme of restoration has taken place at New Lanark, and a visitor centre now provides a first-rate introduction to the mills and village.

PAISLEY, *Strathclyde*

Paisley was the principal cotton textile town in Scotland, particularly notable for the production of shawls and thread. A variety of mills and some blocks of sandstone tenements, which, as in Glasgow, were the traditional homes of Paisley's working people, still stand in the town. The museum and gallery in High Street are the home of the world's best collection of Paisley shawls.

Four miles to the west at Kilbarchan just south of the A761 and north-west of the B787 is a weaver's cottage beautifully restored by the National Trust for Scotland. The cottage illustrates with great clarity the

Cottage industry preserved at Kilbarchan

way of life of domestic textile workers before the era of the great factories, although hand-loom weaving continued on a small scale at Kilbarchan until the 1950s. The cottage was built in 1723 by Andrew John and Jenat Bryden whose names are inscribed over the front door. Of outstanding interest is the basement loom shop which has been furnished with the possessions of a Kilbarchan weaver called Willie Meikle. His loom is in full working order, with all its accessories, and his tartan trousers and waistcoat are displayed with other personal items. Demonstrations of the craft are given three times a week.

PERTH, *Tayside*

Perth, traditionally the 'Gateway to the Highlands', has much to interest the industrial archaeologist. Perth's former waterworks were housed in a spectacular building, a water tank capping a rotunda with a domed roof and Ionic pilasters, all executed in cast iron in 1832 to the design of Adam Anderson. It is now an information centre. On the northern edge of the city just off the A9 is a further visitor centre at the Caithness Glassworks, opened in 1979, where glassblowing can be observed.

About 6 miles north, approached from the A9 and the B9099, is the village of Stanley, which has one of the most important mills complexes in Scotland, begun by Richard Arkwright and partners in 1785 and still in limited production. Bell Mill, which is in brick with a stone plinth, is the oldest mill, and has a pediment, cupola and a staircase turret. The 20-bay, five-storey

Interesting architectural features at the splendid Bell Mill

East Mill was built in 1840, and the 22-bay Mid Mill a few years later. There are several ranges of single-storey buildings, an onion-domed gatehouse and a sluice house in similar style. Houses for the mill workers can be seen in Store Street within the adjacent village.

PRESTONGRANGE, *Lothian*

Prestongrange, on the coast about 6 miles east of Edinburgh, is one of the sites of the Scottish Mining Museum. A visitor centre introduces the site whose chief features are a beam pumping engine built by Harveys of Hayle, which operated from 1874 to 1954, the former colliery power station,

The sturdy beam pumping engine

and a 24-chamber Hoffmann kiln used for the production of bricks, an activity in which many colliery companies became involved.

About 5 miles to the south is the museum's other main site at Lady Victoria Colliery, Newtongrange. The colliery was sunk in 1890 by the Lothian Coal Company, and closed in 1981. Its massive headstock is preserved, and visitors can see the winding engine by Grant Ritchie and Co of Kilmarnock in its white- and grey-tiled engine house. It is still rotated to turn the giant winding drum which raised men and coal from the pit. The method of unloading coal tubs from the cages which conveyed them up the shafts is demonstrated, and there are displays on the history of the colliery. Most of the village of Newtongrange consists of one-and-a-half-storey brick cottages built by the mining company.

SOUTH QUEENSFERRY, *Lothian*

The Forth Bridge is Scotland's most celebrated industrial monument. For many years railway passengers had to cross the Firth of Forth by ferry. By the early 1880s preparations were in hand for a railway bridge to be constructed to the design of Thomas Bouch, but when his Tay Bridge collapsed in 1879 the existing plans were set aside.

A new design by John Fowler and Benjamin Baker for a cantilever bridge was commenced in 1883 and completed in 1890. The bridge is $1\frac{1}{2}$ miles long, with two spans of 521m and two of 210m. It was the first major engineering structure to be built in steel. The best viewing point is on the south side along the B924 to the east of South Queensferry where there is a visitor centre. The adjacent Hawes Pier

The Forth Bridge, a complex engineering challenge

was built by John Rennie and Robert Stevenson in 1809—18, and was used by the ferries. Boat trips to Inchcolm Island provide fine views of the bridge. During most of the day at least two local trains an hour cross the bridge between Dalmeny and North Queensferry stations. The South Queensferry Museum in High Street has displays on the rail and road bridges, ferries and local industries.

UNION CANAL

The Edinburgh and Glasgow Union Canal extended some 30 miles from Port Hopetoun basin in Edinburgh to a junction with the Forth and Clyde Canal at Port Downie near Falkirk. It was built between 1818 and 1822 and for a time was important for passenger as well as freight traffic. Parts of the canal can still be navigated and the well-maintained towpaths provide means of access to some magnificent engineering works. The 587m Falkirk Tunnel near the eastern end is a protected monument. At Causewayend east of Linlithgow on the B825 is the basin where the canal connected with the Slamannan Railway which ran westwards towards Airdrie. In the early 1840s packet boats on the canal competed with coaches at Causewayend to carry passengers travelling between Edinburgh and Glasgow. A short distance to the east is the magnificent 12-arch aqueduct over the River Avon, 247m long and some 26m above the river.

An aqueduct on the Union Canal

The Muiravonside Country Park provides a convenient base for the exploration of this region on foot. In Linlithgow itself the stable block within the canal basin in Manse Road near the railway station contains a small museum relating to the canal, and is also a base for a cruise boat as well as for hire boats of various kinds which can be used to explore the canal.

The basin at Linlithgow, a starting point for boat tours and site of a canal museum

Another fine aqueduct, of five arches and 128m long, crosses the River Almond, and can be approached by a lane leading off junction 2 on the M8 through the Newbridge Industrial Estate. Alternatively this area can be explored along the towpath from the Bridge Inn at Ratho from which a cruise boat operates in season.

The third large aqueduct is the Slateford Aqueduct over the Water of Leith which consists of 14 arches, and runs parallel to the A70 Lanark Road in the western suburbs of Edinburgh. The stone overbridges along the canal are of unfailing elegance, and many of the half-mile posts still survive. The canal provides an entrancing means of exploring one of the most influential regions in the Industrial Revolution in Scotland.

MUSEUMS AND SITES TO VISIT

The following museums, attractions and organisations are, wholly or partially, based on industrial themes. If writing to them for information, please enclose a stamped, addressed envelope.

ABERDULAIS. Aberdulais Falls, *Aberdulais, Neath, W Glamorgan SA10 8EU (0639-56674).*

AMBERLEY. Amberley Chalk Pits Museum, *Houghton Bridge, Amberley, Arundel, W Sussex BN18 9LT (0798-831370).*

ARBROATH. Arbroath Museum, *Signal Tower, Ladyloan, Arbroath, Tayside (0674-75598).*

BAKEWELL. Magpie Mine, *Sheldon, Bakewell, Derbys.*

BATH. Bath Industrial Heritage Centre, *Julian Road, Bath, Avon BH1 2RH (0225-318348).*

BEAMISH. North of England Open-Air Museum, *Beamish, Stanley, Co Durham DH9 0RG (0207-231811).*

BERSHAM. Bersham Industrial Heritage Centre, *Bersham, Wrexham, Clwyd LL14 4HT (0978-261529).*

BEWDLEY. Bewdley Museum, *The Shambles, Load Street, Bewdley, Hereford and Worcs DY12 2AE (0299-403573).* ■ Severn Valley Railway, *Bewdley Station, Bewdley, Hereford and Worcs DY12 1BG (0299-403816).*

BIGGAR. Gasworks Museum, *Biggar, Strathclyde.*

BIRMINGHAM. Birmingham Museum and Art Gallery, *Chamberlain Square, Birmingham B3 3DH (021-235 2834).* ■ Sarehole Mill, *Cokebank Road, Hall Green, Birmingham B13 0BD (021-777 6612).* ■ Birmingham Museum of Science and Industry, *Newhall Street, Birmingham B3 1RZ (021-236 1022).* ■ Birmingham Railway Museum, 670 Warwick Road, *Tyseley, Birmingham B11 2HL (021-707 4696).*

BLAENAU FFESTINIOG. Ffestiniog Railway, *Harbour Station, Porthmadog, Gwynedd LL49 9NF (0766-512340).* ■ Llechwedd Slate Caverns, *Blaenau Ffestiniog, Gwynedd LL41 3NB (0766-830306).* ■ Gloddfa Ganol, *Blaenau Ffestiniog, Gwynedd LL41 3NB (0766-830664).*

BONAWE. Ironworks, *Bonawe, nr Oban, Strathclyde (08662-432).*

BO'NESS. Kinneil Museum, *Duchess Anne Cottages, Kinneil Estate, Bo'Ness, Central.* ■ Scottish Railway Preservation Society, *Bo'Ness and Kinneil Railway Centre, Union Street, Bo'Ness, Central (0506-822298).*

BRADFORD. Bradford Industrial Museum, *Moorside Road, Eccleshill, Bradford BD2 2HP (0274-631756).*

BRISTOL. City of Bristol Museum and Art Gallery, *Queens Road, Bristol BS8 1RL (0272-299771).* ■ SS Great Britain, *Great Western Dock, Gas Ferry Road, Bristol BS1 6TY (0272-260680).*

BURTON UPON TRENT. Bass Museum of Brewing History, *Horninglow Street, Burton upon Trent, Staffs (0283-45301).*

CARDIFF. Welsh Folk Museum, *St Fagans, Cardiff CF5 6XB (0222-569441).* ■ Welsh Industrial and Maritime Museum, *Bute Street, Cardiff CF1 6AN (0222-481919).*

CHATHAM. Chatham Historic Dockyard, *The Old Pay Office, Church Lane, Chatham, Kent ME4 4TE (0634-812551).*

COVENTRY. Herbert Art Gallery and Museum, *Jordan Well, Coventry (0203-833333/832381).*

CRICH. The National Tramway Museum, *Crich, Matlock, Derby DE4 5DP (077385-2562).*

CROMFORD. The Arkwright Society, *Cromford Mill, Mill Lane, Cromford, Derby DE4 3RR (062982-4297).*

DERBY. Derby Industrial Museum, *The Silk Mill, Derby DE1 3AR (0332-293111, ext 740).*

DIDCOT. The Great Western Society, *Didcot Railway Centre, Didcot, Oxon OX11 7NJ (0235-817200).*

DOLAUCOTHI. Dolaucothi Gold Mines, *Pumpsaint, Llanwrda, Dyfed (05585-359).*

DRE-FACH FELINDRE. Museum of the Welsh Woollen Industry, *Dre-fach Felindre, Llandysul, Dyfed (0559-370929).*

DUDDON. Duddon Furnace, *c/o Lake District National Park Information Service, Bank House, High Street, Windermere, Cumbria (09662-2498).*

An underground ride through old workings on an electric-powered tram at the Llechwedd Slate Caverns, Blaenau Ffestiniog

DUDLEY. The Black Country Museum, *Tipton Road, Dudley, W Midlands DY1 4SQ (021-557 9643).*

DUNDEE. Dundee Art Galleries and Museums, *Albert Square, Dundee DD1 1DA (0382-23141).*

EDINBURGH. Royal Museum of Scotland, *Chambers Street, Edinburgh EH1 1JF (031-225 7534).*

ELLESMERE PORT. The Boat Museum, *Dockyard Road, Ellesmere Port, Cheshire L65 4EF (051-355 5017).*

EXETER. Royal Albert Memorial Museum, *Queen Street, Exeter, Devon EX4 3RX (0392-265858).* ■ Exeter Maritime Museum, *Isca Ltd, The Haven, Exeter, Devon EX2 8DT (0392- 58075).*

FAVERSHAM. Fleur-de-Lis Heritage Centre, *Preston Street, Faversham, Kent (0795-534542).*

FLEETWOOD. Museum of the Fishing Industry, *Dock Street, Fleetwood, Lancs FY7 6AQ (03917-66211).*

FOREST OF DEAN. Dean Heritage Centre, *Camp Mill, Soudley, Cinderford, Glos GL14 7UG (0594-22170).*

GLASGOW. Museum of Transport, *Kelvin Hall, 1 Bunhouse Road, Glasgow G3 8DP (041-357 3929).* ■ People's Palace Museum, *Glasgow Green, Glasgow G40 1AT (041-554 0223).*

This Scottish veteran, the Arrol-Johnston TT Model '18' is on display at Glasgow's Museum of Transport

GLOUCESTER. The Robert Opie Collection-Museum of Packaging and Advertising, *Albert Warehouse, Gloucester Docks, Gloucester GL1 2EH (0452-302309).* ■ National Waterways Museum, *Llanthony Warehouse, Gloucester Docks, Gloucester GL1 2EH (0452-25524).*

HEADS OF VALLEYS. Torfaen Museum Trust, *Park Buildings, Pontypool, Gwent NP4 6JH (04955-52036).* ■ Big Pit Mining Museum, *Blaenavon, Gwent NP4 9XP (0495-790311).* ■ Cyfarthfa Castle, *Cyfarthfa Park, Merthyr Tydfil, Mid Glamorgan (0685-723112).* ■ Cefn Coed Mining Museum, *Blaenant Colliery, Crynant, Neath, W Glamorgan SA10 8SN (0639-750556).*

HELMSHORE. Museum of the Lancashire Textile Industry, *Holcombe Road, Helmshore, Rossendale, Lancs BB4 4NP (0706-226459).*

HOLYWELL. Visitor Centre, Greenfield Valley Heritage Park, *Greenfield, Holywell, Clwyd CH8 7QB (0352-714172).*

IRONBRIDGE. Ironbridge Gorge Museum Trust Ltd, *Ironbridge, Telford, Salop TF8 7AW (095245-3522).*

KILLHOPE. Information on ore-crushing mill *c/o County Planning Dept, County Hall, Durham DH1 5UF (0385-64411, ext 2354).*

LEEDS. Leeds Industrial Museum, *Armley Mills, Canal Road, Armley, Leeds LS1 2EH (0532-637861).*

LEISTON. The Long Shop, *Main Street, Leiston, Suffolk (0728-832189/830530).*

LINLITHGOW. Union Canal Society Museum, *Manse Road Basin, Linlithgow, Lothian (050684-4730).*

LIVERPOOL. Merseyside County Museums, *William Brown Street, Liverpool L3 8EN (051-207 0001/5451).* ■Merseyside Maritime Museum, *Albert Dock, Liverpool L3 1DN (051-709 1551).*

LLANBERIS. The Welsh Slate Museum, *Gilfach Ddu, Llanberis, Gwynedd LL55 4TY (0286-870630).*

LONDON. The Science Museum, *Exhibition Road, London SW7 2DD (01-589 3456).* ■ Museum of London, *London Wall, London EC2Y 5HN (01-600 3699).* ■ Kew Bridge Engines Trust and Water Supply Museum, *Green Dragon Lane, Brentford, Middlesex TW8 0EN (01-568 4757).*

MACCLESFIELD. Macclesfield Heritage Centre, *Roe Street, Macclesfield, Cheshire SK11 6UT (0625-613210).* ■ Paradise Mill, *Park Lane, Macclesfield, Cheshire SK11 6TJ (0625-618228).*

MANCHESTER. Greater Manchester Museum of Science and Industry, *Lower Byrom Street, off Liverpool Road, Castlefield, Manchester M3 4JP (061-832 2244).*

MATLOCK BATH. Peak District Mining Museum/Magpie Mine, *The Pavilion, Matlock Bath, Derby (0629-3834).*

MORWELLHAM. Morwellham Quay Open-Air Museum, *Morwellham, Tavistock, Devon PL19 8JL (0822-832766).*

NEWBY BRIDGE. Stott Park Bobbin Mill, *Finisthwaite, nr Newby Bridge, Cumbria (0448-31087).*

NEWCASTLE UPON TYNE. Museum of Science and Engineering, *Blandford House, Blandford Square, Newcastle upon Tyne NE1 4JA (091-232 6789).*

NEW LANARK. New Lanark Conservation Trust, *New Lanark Mills, Lanark, Strathclyde ML11 9DB (0555-61345).*

NEWTOWN. Newtown Textile Museum, *7 Commercial Street, Newtown, Powys.* ■ Robert Owen Memorial Museum, *The Cross, Broad Street, Newtown, Powys.*

NORTHWICH. The Salt Museum, *162 London Road, Northwich, Cheshire CW9 8AB (0606-41331).*

NORWICH. Castle Museum, *Castle Meadow, Norwich NR1 3JU (0603-611277).* ■ Colman's Mustard Museum, *3 Bridewell Alley, Norwich NR2 1AQ (0603-660166).*

NOTTINGHAM. Castle Museum, *The Castle, Nottingham NG1 6EL (0602-483504).* ■ Nottingham Industrial Museum, *Courtyard Buildings, Wollaton Park, Nottingham NG8 2AE (0602-284602).* ■ Canal Museum, *Canal Street, Nottingham (0602-598835).* ■ Papplewick Pumping Station, *off Longdale Lane, Ravenshead, nr Nottingham NG15 9AJ (0602-632938).* ■ Ruddington Framework Knitters' Shops Preservation Trust, *Ruddington, Nottingham (0602-846914).*

PAISLEY. Museum and Art Galleries, *High Street, Paisley, Strathclyde PA1 2BA (041-889 3151).* ■ Weaver's Cottage, The Cross, Kilbarchan, nr Paisley, *Strathclyde (05057-5588).*

PERTH. Caithness Glass, *Inveralmond, Perth PH1 3TZ (0738-37373).*

PONTYPRIDD. Pontypridd Historical and Cultural Centre, *Bridge Street, Pontypridd, Mid Glamorgan (0443-402077).*

PORTSMOUTH. Portsmouth City Museum and Art Gallery, *Museum Road, Old Portsmouth, Hants PO1 2LJ (0705-827261). Museum also has information on Eastney Pumping Station.*

PORT SUNLIGHT. Heritage Centre, *PO Box 98, Greendale Road, Port Sunlight, Merseyside (051-644 6466).*

PRESTONGRANGE. Scottish Mining Museum - contact Lady Victoria Colliery, *Newtongrange, Lothian EH22 4QN (031-663 7519).*

REDRUTH. Cornish Engines, *East Pool, Cambourne, nr Redruth, Cornwall (0209-216657/715406).*

RYHOPE. Ryhope Engines Museum, *Ryhope Pumping Station, Ryhope, Sunderland, Tyne and Wear.*

ST AUSTELL. Wheal Martyn Museum, *Carthew, St Austell, Cornwall PL26 8XG (0726-850362).*

SHEFFIELD. Sheffield Industrial Museum *(Kelham Island),* *Alma Street, Sheffield S3 8RY (0742-722106).* ■ Abbeydale Industrial Hamlet, *Abbeydale Road South, Sheffield S7 2GW (0742-367731).*
SHREWSBURY. Rowley's House Museum, *Barker Street, Shrewsbury, Salop SY1 1QT (0743-61196).*

George Stephenson's bridge of 1825, built to cross the River Gaunless, Co Durham, is now one of the outside exhibits at York's National Railway Museum

SINGLETON. Weald and Downland Open-Air Museum, *Singleton, Chichester, W Sussex PO18 0EU (0243-63348).*
SOUTHAMPTON. Southampton City Museums and Art Gallery, *Civic Centre, Southampton SO9 4XF (0703-223855).*
SOUTH QUEENSFERRY. South Queensferry Museum, *High Street, South Queensferry, Lothian.*
STOKE-ON-TRENT. City Museum and Art Gallery, *Bethesda Street, Hanley, Stoke-on-Trent ST1 3DE (0782-202173). Museum also has information on Etruscan Bone Mills.* ■ Gladstone Pottery Museum, *26 Uttoxeter Road, Longton, Stoke-on-Trent ST3 1PQ (0782-319232).* ■ Chatterley Whitfield Mining Museum, *Tunstall, Stoke-on-Trent ST6 8UN (0782-813337).* ■Wedgwood Centre, *Josiah Wedgwood and Sons Ltd, Barlaston, Stoke-on-Trent ST12 9ES (078139-3218/4141).*
STOURBRIDGE. Broadfield House Glass Museum, *Barnett Lane, Kingswinford, W Midlands DY6 9QA (0384-273011).* ■ Red House Glassworks, *Stuart Crystal, Wordsley, Stourbridge, W Midlands DY8 4AA (0384-71161).*
STROUD VALLEY. Stroud District (Cowle) Museum, *Lansdown, Stroud, Glos GL5 1BB (04536-3394).*
STYAL. Quarry Bank Mill, *Styal, Cheshire SK9 4LA (0625-527468).*
SWANSEA. Swansea Maritime and Industrial Museum, *Museum Square, Maritime Quarter, South Dock, Swansea, W Glamorgan SA1 1SN (0792-50351/470371).*
SWINDON. Great Western Railway Museum, *Faringdon Road, Swindon SN1 5BJ (0793-26161).*
WAKEFIELD. Yorkshire Mining Museum, *Caphouse Colliery, New Road, Overton, Wakefield, W Yorks WF4 4AH (0924-484806).*
WANLOCKHEAD. Museum of Scottish Lead Mining, *Goldscaur Row, Wanlockhead, Dumfries and Galloway (0659-74387).*
YORK. National Railway Museum, *Leeman Road, York YO2 4XJ (0904-621261).* ■ York Castle Museum, *The Eye of York, York YO1 1RY (0904-53611).*

The national organisation for the study of industrial heritage is the *Association for Industrial Archaeology, Ironbridge Gorge Museum, Ironbridge, Telford, Salop TF8 7AW.*

FURTHER READING

Alderton, D and Booker, J. *The Batsford Guide to the Industrial Archaeology of East Anglia.* Batsford (1980).

Ashmore, O. *The Industrial Archaeology of North-West England.* Manchester University Press (1982).

Atkinson, F. *The Industrial Archaeology of North-East England.* David and Charles (1974).

Brook, F. *The Industrial Archaeology of the British Isles: the West Midlands.* Batsford (1977).

Buchanan, C R and R A. *The Batsford Guide to the Industrial Archaeology of Central Southern Scotland.* Batsford (1980).

Butt, J. *The Industrial Archaeology of Scotland.* David and Charles (1967).

Cossons, N. *The B P Book of Industrial Archaeology (Second Edition).* David and Charles (1987).

Falconer, K. *Guide to England's Industrial Heritage.* Batsford (1980).

Haselfoot, A J. *The Batsford Guide to the Industrial Archaeology of South-East England.* Batsford (1978).

Hudson, K. *The Industrial Archaeology of Southern England.* David and Charles (1965).

Minchinton, W. *A Guide to Industrial Archaeology Sites in Britain.* Paladin, Granada (1984).

Morgan Rees, D. *The Industrial Archaeology of Wales.* David and Charles (1975).

Smith, D. *The Industrial Archaeology of the East Midlands.* David and Charles (1965).

Trinder, B. *The Making of the Industrial Landscape.* Dent (1982). Paperback Edition Alan Sutton (1987).

Vialls, C. *Your Book of Industrial Archaeology.* Faber (1981).

INDEX

Page numbers for major gazetteer entries appear in **bold**.
(Please note: museums are only indexed when their titles do not include a placename, eg Bass Museum of Brewing. For other museums, eg Bath Industrial Heritage Centre, see Bath entry).